£2.00

CW01370141

Copyright © 2023

All rights reserved.

ISBN:
ISBN-13:

Table of Contents

Unsung Heroines of Scientific Discovery
Rosalind Franklin: The Unsung DNA Pioneer 7

Mary Anning: Fossil Hunter Extraordinaire..8

Lise Meitner: A Nuclear Pioneer 9

Chien-Shiung Wu: The First Lady of Physics 11

Women Innovators: Breaking Barriers in Technology
Ada Lovelace: The First Computer Programmer...13

Grace Hopper: Pioneer of Computer Programming Languages 14

Hedy Lamarr: Inventor and Actress 16

Katherine Johnson: Trailblazing Mathematician at NASA 18

Radia Perlman: Inventor of Spanning Tree Protocol 19

Trailblazers in Mathematics and Logic
Emmy Noether: Revolutionizing Abstract Algebra 22

Hypatia of Alexandria: Scholar of Ancient Mathematics 23

Sophie Germain: Pioneer in Number Theory..25

Forgotten Artists: Masterpieces from the Shadows
Artemisia Gentileschi: A Renaissance Painter Resurfaced.........................28

Amrita Sher-Gil: Reclaiming Identity through Art......................................29

Hilma af Klint: Pioneering Abstract Art 31

Lee Krasner: A Trailblazer of Abstract Expressionism................................32

Sofonisba Anguissola: Renaissance Painter of Royal Courts......................34

Women Writers: Amplifying Voices through Literature
Charlotte Perkins Gilman: Challenging Gender Roles through Literature ..36

Zora Neale Hurston: Celebrating African-American Culture and Folklore..37

Nella Larsen: Pioneering African-American Novelist of the Harlem Renaissance 39

George Eliot: Challenging Gender Expectations in Victorian England 41

Djuna Barnes: Exploring Experimental Fiction and Modernist Literature .. 43

Musicians and Composers: Orchestrating Change

Clara Schumann: Virtuoso Pianist and Composer of the Romantic Era 45

Billie Holiday: Transforming Jazz with Emotional Depth and Social Commentary 46

Fanny Mendelssohn: A Hidden Voice of Romantic Music 47

Nina Simone: Empowering Voice for Civil Rights and Musical Innovation. 49

Rosa Parks: The Mother of the Civil Rights Movement 52

Visionaries of Social Justice Movements

Malala Yousafzai: Champion of Education and Girls' Rights 53

Dolores Huerta: Advocate for Farmworkers' Rights and Latinx Empowerment 55

Audre Lorde: Intersectional Feminist and Literary Trailblazer 56

Wangari Maathai: Environmentalist and Women's Rights Advocate 57

Women Warriors: Challenging Gender Norms

Nakano Takeko: Fearless Samurai Warrior of Feudal Japan 60

Queen Tamar: Fierce Ruler and Military Strategist of Georgia 61

Khutulun: Mongolian Wrestler Princess and Military Strategist 64

Lakshmi Bai: The Rani of Jhansi and Symbol of Indian Resistance 65

Trailblazing Politicians and Diplomats

Sirimavo Bandaranaike: World's First Female Prime Minister 68

Jeannette Rankin: First Woman Elected to the United States Congress 69

Madeleine Albright: Diplomatic Trailblazer and First Female U.S. Secretary of State 71

Golda Meir: Iron Lady and Israel's First Female Prime Minister 72

Vigdís Finnbogadóttir: Pioneering President and Global Advocate for Women 73

Hidden Figures: Women in the Shadow of War
Codebreakers of Bletchley Park: Breaking Enigma's Secrets 77

Rosie the Riveters: Women in Manufacturing and Industry....................... 78

Night Witches: Fearless Women Pilots of the Soviet Union 80

Women Airforce Service Pilots (WASP): Wings for the United States 81

The Radio Operators and Resistance Fighters: Silent Heroes of Espionage 83

Overcoming Odds: Inspiring Stories of Triumph
Malala Yousafzai: Voice for Girls' Education and Nobel Laureate 85

Helen Keller: Overcoming Deaf-Blindness to Inspire the World................ 86

Harriet Tubman: Abolitionist, Freedom Fighter, and Underground Railroad Conductor 88

Junko Tabei: Conquering Everest and Breaking Gender Barriers 90

Maya Angelou: Poet, Author, and Voice of Resilience 91

Trailblazers in Sports and Athletics
Wilma Rudolph: Triumph over Adversity in Track and Field 94

Althea Gibson: The First African American Grand Slam Champion 95

Babe Didrikson Zaharias: Multisport Champion and Barrier Breaker 97

Gertrude Ederle: The First Woman to Swim the English Channel 99

Alice Coachman: Trailblazer in Olympic Track and Field 100

Women of Color: Reclaiming Their Narratives
Sojourner Truth: Activist and Abolitionist 104

Frida Kahlo: The Unyielding Spirit of Mexican Art 105

Shirley Chisholm: Pioneering Politician and Advocate for Equality 107

Maya Angelou: Voice of Strength and Resilience 108

Patsy Mink: Champion for Women's Rights and Education 109

Amplifying Indigenous Voices
Malinche: Interpreting Cultures and Indigenous Identity......................... 112

Winona LaDuke: Environmental Activism and Indigenous Rights 114

Buffy Sainte-Marie: Artistic Expression and Cultural Advocacy 115

Wilma Mankiller: Leadership and Empowerment in Cherokee Nation.... 117

Patricia Michaels: Indigenous Fashion and Cultural Revitalization 118

Lost Queens and Empresses
Hatshepsut: The Female Pharaoh of Ancient Egypt 122

Wu Zetian: Empress of China's Tang Dynasty 123

Rani Padmini: Queen of Mewar and Symbol of Courage 125

Zenobia: Queen of Palmyra and Warrior Queen 126

Theodora: Empress of the Byzantine Empire 127

Women in Ancient History: Shattering Myths
Cleopatra: Queen of Egypt and Political Strategist 130

Enheduanna: High Priestess and Earliest Known Female Author 132

Boudicca: Warrior Queen of the Iceni Tribe.. 133

Sappho: Poetess of Ancient Greece 134

Agnodice: Pioneer Female Physician in Ancient Athens 136

PART ONE

PIONEERS OF SCIENCE AND INNOVATION

1.1 UNSUNG HEROINES OF SCIENTIFIC DISCOVERY

Rosalind Franklin: The Unsung DNA Pioneer

Rosalind Franklin was a British biophysicist and chemist who conducted groundbreaking research on the molecular structure of DNA in the early 1950s. Using X-ray crystallography, which involves directing X-rays at crystallized DNA samples, Franklin captured crucial images that provided critical insights into its molecular structure.

Her work produced high-resolution X-ray diffraction images, most notably Photograph 51. This image, obtained through meticulous experimental techniques and analysis, showed a distinct cross-shaped diffraction pattern that hinted at the presence of a helical configuration within the DNA molecule.

Franklin's X-ray crystallography work provided valuable data that James Watson and Francis Crick later used at the University of Cambridge to construct their famous model of the DNA double helix. However, it is important to note that Franklin's work and findings were obtained without her knowledge or consent, as her research had been shared with Watson and Crick without her permission.

Despite her significant contributions, Franklin's role in discovering the DNA structure was initially overlooked and undervalued. Her male colleagues, Watson and Crick, who were awarded the Nobel Prize in Physiology or Medicine in 1962 for their discovery, did not acknowledge her crucial contributions in their initial publications. Only after her untimely death in 1958 did her work receive more recognition and appreciation.

There has been a growing recognition of Rosalind Franklin's pivotal role in discovering DNA's structure in recent years. Her X-ray crystallography data and analyses laid the foundation for our understanding of the double helix structure, and her contributions have become increasingly acknowledged and celebrated in the scientific community.

Rosalind Franklin's work not only advanced our understanding of DNA but also paved the way for further research and advancements in genetics, molecular biology, and biotechnology. Her story serves as a powerful reminder of the importance of recognizing and honoring the contributions of women in scientific discoveries, even in cases where their work may have been overshadowed or underappreciated.

Mary Anning: Fossil Hunter Extraordinaire

Mary Anning, a self-taught paleontologist from the 19th century, made significant contributions to paleontology despite facing numerous challenges and societal constraints. Her discoveries played a crucial role in advancing our understanding of prehistoric life and laid the groundwork for modern paleontological research.

Born in 1799 in Lyme Regis, a coastal town in England, Mary Anning developed a deep passion for fossil hunting from a young age. Growing up in a working-class family, Anning and her father collected fossils along the cliffs and shores of Lyme Regis to sell them as curiosities to tourists.

Anning's exceptional observational skills and keen eye for fossils quickly became apparent. She made her first significant discovery at the age of 12 when she unearthed a complete skeleton of an Ichthyosaur, an extinct marine reptile. This find garnered attention and acclaim, establishing her as a remarkable fossil collector.

Over the years, Mary Anning continued to make groundbreaking discoveries. She unearthed numerous fossil specimens, including complete skeletons of Ichthyosaurs, Plesiosaurs, and Pterosaurs, as well as various fossilized fish and ammonites. These findings were instrumental in expanding scientific knowledge about ancient marine life during the early 19th century.

Despite her significant contributions to the field, Anning faced numerous challenges. As a woman and member of the working class, she encountered gender and class biases that restricted her access to academic institutions and scientific societies. These limitations prevented her from receiving formal recognition and hindered her ability to publish her findings.

Nonetheless, Anning's work attracted the attention and collaboration of several eminent scientists, who acknowledged her expertise and relied on her knowledge. Notably, her correspondence and cooperation with geologists such as Henry De la Beche and William Buckland contributed to the development of paleontological theories and helped shape the emerging field of geology.

Mary Anning's contributions to paleontology paved the way for groundbreaking scientific advancements. Her discoveries challenged prevailing notions about extinct species, deepened understanding of ancient ecosystems, and provided valuable insights into Earth's geological history.

Furthermore, Anning's work shattered gender and social barriers in the scientific community, inspiring future generations of women in science. Her determination, resilience, and commitment to pursuing knowledge in the face of adversity serve as an enduring testament to her legacy.

Lise Meitner: A Nuclear Pioneer

An Austrian physicist, Lise Meitner made significant contributions to nuclear physics, particularly in her collaboration with Otto Hahn, which led to the landmark discovery of nuclear fission. Their work revolutionized our understanding of atomic structure and had profound implications for both scientific research and practical applications.

Lise Meitner and Otto Hahn began their collaboration in the 1920s when they worked together at the Kaiser Wilhelm Institute in Berlin. Their research focused on the study of radioactivity and the behavior of atomic nuclei. Meitner's expertise in theoretical physics complemented Hahn's practical skills, making them a formidable scientific duo.

Their most notable breakthrough came in 1938 when they conducted experiments involving the bombardment of uranium atoms with neutrons. During their investigations, Meitner astutely analyzed the results and recognized that the nucleus of the uranium atom had been split into two smaller fragments, releasing an enormous amount of energy. This groundbreaking process came to be known as nuclear fission.

Meitner and her nephew Otto Frisch further developed the theoretical framework to explain the phenomenon of nuclear fission. They proposed that the energy released during fission resulted from the conversion of mass into energy, as described by Einstein's famous equation, $E=mc^2$. This realization laid the foundation for understanding the immense power that could be harnessed from nuclear reactions.

However, despite her significant contributions, Meitner's role in discovering nuclear fission was overshadowed at the time. In 1938, she was forced to flee Nazi Germany due to her Jewish heritage, and she continued her research in Stockholm, Sweden. It was there that she collaborated closely with Otto Frisch and shared her insights on nuclear fission.

Meanwhile, Otto Hahn, who remained in Germany, continued his experimental work and published a paper in 1939 that described the experimental evidence of nuclear fission. The paper did not explicitly credit Meitner for her theoretical contributions.

In later years, Meitner's pivotal role in discovering nuclear fission gained recognition, and she was acknowledged for her groundbreaking insights. In 1966, she was awarded the prestigious Enrico Fermi Award for her contributions to nuclear physics.

The discovery of nuclear fission by Meitner and Hahn had far-reaching consequences. It laid the groundwork for the development of atomic energy, leading to advancements in nuclear power generation and nuclear weapons technology. Additionally, their work opened up new avenues of research in understanding the fundamental nature of matter and energy.

Lise Meitner's contribution to nuclear physics goes beyond the specific discovery of nuclear fission. She was a trailblazer for women in science, overcoming societal and professional barriers to make significant advancements in a male-dominated field. Her perseverance, intellect, and collaboration with Otto Hahn paved the way for groundbreaking discoveries and continue to inspire scientists today.

Chien-Shiung Wu: The First Lady of Physics

Chien-Shiung Wu was a Chinese-American physicist who conducted groundbreaking research in nuclear physics. Her work, notably the Wu experiment, played a pivotal role in verifying the violation of the principle of parity and challenging established theories in particle physics.

In the 1950s, Chien-Shiung Wu conducted her research at Columbia University in New York under the guidance of physicist Tsung-Dao Lee. At the time, there was a widely accepted principle in physics called the principle of parity conservation, which stated that the laws of physics should remain unchanged if the coordinate system is reflected.

However, Wu and her colleagues, Tsung-Dao Lee and Chen-Ning Yang, proposed a bold experiment to test the conservation of parity in weak nuclear interactions. They hypothesized that the weak force responsible for certain types of radioactive decay might violate the principle of parity conservation.

In 1956, Wu conducted what would come to be known as the Wu experiment or the Wu-Hasegawa-Mueller experiment. The experiment involved studying the beta decay of cobalt-60 nuclei, a process in which a neutron inside the nucleus transforms into a proton, emitting an electron and an antineutrino. Wu designed the experiment to measure the distribution of emitted electrons relative to the spin orientation of the cobalt-60 nuclei.

The groundbreaking result of the Wu experiment confirmed that the weak nuclear force violated the principle of parity conservation. Wu and her colleagues observed a significant asymmetry in the emission of electrons, depending on the orientation of the cobalt-60 nuclei's spin. This result overturned the long-standing assumption that the weak nuclear force respected parity conservation.

The Wu experiment had profound implications for particle physics and our understanding of the fundamental forces governing the universe. It challenged established theories and provided evidence that the weak force distinguishes between left-handed and right-handed particles, violating parity symmetry.

Wu's experiment garnered significant attention and recognition within the scientific community. It also contributed to Lee and Yang receiving the 1957 Nobel Prize in Physics for their work on parity non-conservation, with Wu's crucial experimental contributions acknowledged.

Chien-Shiung Wu's pioneering research in the Wu experiment revealed the violation of the principle of parity in weak nuclear interactions and demonstrated the importance of experimental precision and design in particle physics. Her work paved the way for further investigations into the fundamental symmetries of nature and had a lasting impact on the field.

Additionally, Wu's accomplishments shattered gender barriers in physics. She became known as the "First Lady of Physics" and inspired generations of women in science with her exceptional intellect, dedication, and groundbreaking contributions to the field of nuclear physics.

1.2 WOMEN INNOVATORS: BREAKING BARRIERS IN TECHNOLOGY

Ada Lovelace: The First Computer Programmer

Ada Lovelace, born Augusta Ada Byron in 1815, was an English mathematician and writer known for her work with Charles Babbage and her significant contributions to computer science. While often referred to as the world's first computer programmer, it is important to understand the context and her specific accomplishments.

During the 19th century, Charles Babbage conceived the idea of a mechanical general-purpose computer known as the Analytical Engine. Babbage's machine was a precursor to modern computers, capable of performing various calculations and operations using punched cards. Ada Lovelace became acquainted with Babbage and his work, and she recognized the potential of the Analytical Engine far beyond mere calculation.

Lovelace corresponded with Babbage and immersed herself in studying the engine's design and capabilities. In 1842, she translated an article about Babbage's Analytical Engine by Italian mathematician Luigi Menabrea. However, Lovelace went beyond a mere translation and added extensive notes and explanations of her own. These notes, which ended up being longer than the original article, included what is now considered the first published algorithm intended to be executed by a machine.

Lovelace's designed her algorithm to calculate a sequence of Bernoulli numbers using Babbage's Analytical Engine. However, how she described and conceptualized the process made her work significant. Lovelace recognized that the Analytical Engine could manipulate numbers, symbols, and other forms of data, which led her to envision the machine's potential for tasks beyond calculation. She foresaw the possibility of programming the engine to create music, produce graphics, and even generate original art and literature.

Lovelace's visionary insights demonstrated an understanding of the fundamental principles of computing, including the concept of a general-purpose machine capable of executing various tasks through a sequence of instructions. Her work challenged the notion that Babbage's machine was limited to numerical calculations.

While Lovelace's contributions were significant, it is worth noting that the Analytical Engine itself was never fully realized or built during her lifetime. The machine remained a theoretical concept, and Lovelace's notes and ideas were primarily overlooked and forgotten until they were rediscovered and recognized for their importance in the mid-20th century.

Nevertheless, Ada Lovelace's work and ideas have profoundly impacted the development of computer science and the understanding of the capabilities of computers. Her recognition as the first computer programmer is a testament to her visionary thinking and the lasting relevance of her contributions to the field.

Grace Hopper: Pioneer of Computer Programming Languages

Grace Hopper, born Grace Brewster Murray in 1906, was an American computer scientist and naval officer who significantly contributed to computer programming languages. Her work was instrumental in shaping the development of modern programming and making computers more user-friendly and accessible.

Hopper's early career was marked by her involvement with the Harvard Mark I computer, one of the earliest electromechanical computers. She worked as a programmer on the Mark I and gained valuable experience in computer programming during this time. Hopper's talent for programming and her innovative approach to problem-solving soon became evident.

In the 1950s, Hopper joined the team at the Eckert-Mauchly Computer Corporation, where she worked on developing the UNIVAC I computer. During this period, she became increasingly frustrated with the lack of standardized programming languages. At the time, programming computers was a complex and time-consuming task, requiring intimate knowledge of the computer's hardware and low-level machine language instructions.

Hopper recognized the need for a programming language that would be more accessible and business-oriented, allowing non-technical users to write computer programs. This vision led her to work on developing COBOL (Common Business-Oriented Language) in the late 1950s. COBOL was designed to be easily readable and understood by business professionals, allowing them to write programs without having to delve into the intricacies of machine code.

Hopper's efforts to create COBOL were met with resistance and skepticism from some in the computing community. However, she persisted in her advocacy for the language and worked diligently to promote its adoption. Her efforts paid off, and COBOL became one of the most widely used programming languages in the business world. It revolutionized computer programming by providing a high-level language that made it easier for programmers to write and maintain code.

Beyond her work on COBOL, Hopper also played a crucial role in the development of compiler technology. She coined the term "compiler" and was involved in creating the first compiler, which translated high-level programming languages into machine code that computers could execute. This breakthrough eliminated the need for programmers to write machine code manually and significantly accelerated the development process.

Hopper's contributions to computer programming languages were not only technical but also cultural. She was a strong advocate for standardization and worked tirelessly to promote the adoption of programming languages across different computer systems. Her efforts helped establish a foundation for collaboration and interoperability in the field of computing.

Throughout her career, Hopper remained actively involved in the computing community and continued to make significant contributions. She served in the U.S. Navy Reserves, rising to the rank of Rear Admiral and becoming a respected leader and mentor for many aspiring computer scientists.

Grace Hopper's pioneering work in computer programming languages and her commitment to making computers more accessible and user-friendly have impacted the field of computer science. Her contributions laid the foundation for modern programming and opened the doors for a broader range of users to harness the power of computers. She is widely recognized as a trailblazer and a true pioneer in the world of computing.

Hedy Lamarr: Inventor and Actress

Hedy Lamarr, born Hedwig Eva Maria Kiesler in 1914, was a prominent actress during Hollywood's Golden Age. However, her contributions to technology go beyond her successful acting career. Alongside composer George Antheil, Lamarr played a pivotal role in developing a groundbreaking technology known as frequency-hopping spread spectrum (FHSS) during World War II.

At the time, the world was embroiled in the conflict of World War II, and Lamarr wanted to contribute to the war effort in a meaningful way. Drawing from her interest in science and technology, Lamarr recognized the significance of radio-controlled torpedoes and sought to improve their effectiveness by developing a more secure means of communication.

Lamarr and Antheil collaborated to devise a solution to prevent enemy forces from jamming the radio signals guiding the torpedoes. They developed the concept of a frequency-hopping spread spectrum, which involved rapidly changing the transmitted signal's frequency synchronized between the sender and receiver.

The idea behind FHSS was to make it extremely difficult for an adversary to intercept or interfere with the communication by constantly changing the frequency. This approach made the signal more resilient to jamming and interception, enhancing the security and reliability of radio communications.

In 1942, Lamarr and Antheil received a patent for their invention titled "Secret Communication System," which detailed the concept of frequency hopping. However, their groundbreaking technology did not immediately gain recognition or implementation during the war.

It was not until the 1960s, with the rediscovery of the FHSS concept, that its true potential was realized. The development of digital communication systems and the advent of modern wireless technologies created an environment where Lamarr's invention could flourish.

Today, Lamarr's frequency-hopping spread spectrum serves as a precursor to several vital wireless communication technologies. The principles she and Antheil developed have been instrumental in developing modern technologies like Wi-Fi, Bluetooth, and other wireless communication protocols. These technologies rely on the same fundamental concept of rapidly changing frequencies to enhance security, minimize interference, and enable robust communication over the airwaves.

Despite her significant technological contribution, Lamarr's work in this field remained largely unrecognized for many years. However, in the later stages of her life, she received due recognition for her contributions. In 1997, she was honored with the Electronic Frontier Foundation Pioneer Award, and in 2014, she was posthumously inducted into the National Inventors Hall of Fame for her invention of the frequency-hopping spread spectrum.

Hedy Lamarr's story serves as a reminder that talent and innovation can transcend traditional boundaries. Her groundbreaking work in the entertainment industry and technology showcases her remarkable intellect and impact on shaping the modern world. She stands as an inspiring figure, demonstrating that women can excel in fields traditionally dominated by men and contribute significantly to scientific and technological advancements.

Katherine Johnson: Trailblazing Mathematician at NASA

Katherine Johnson, born Katherine Coleman in 1918, was an exceptional African-American mathematician who made groundbreaking contributions to NASA's space missions, particularly during the early days of the U.S. space program. Her calculations and analytical skills were instrumental in the success of crewed space flights and played a pivotal role in the historic Apollo 11 moon landing.

Johnson's journey at NASA began in 1953 when she joined the West Area Computers, a segregated unit of African-American female mathematicians at the National Advisory Committee for Aeronautics (NACA), which later became NASA. Despite facing racial and gender discrimination, Johnson's talent and dedication quickly made her indispensable to the organization.

Johnson's work involved performing complex calculations for various space missions, including trajectory analysis, launch windows, and reentry paths. Her contributions were critical in ensuring the accuracy and safety of space missions. She was known for her precision and attention to detail, earning the trust and respect of her colleagues and superiors.

One of Johnson's most significant contributions came during the Apollo program, the ambitious effort to land humans on the moon. She played a vital role in calculating the trajectory for the Apollo 11 mission, which successfully carried Neil Armstrong and Buzz Aldrin to the lunar surface on July 20, 1969. Johnson's calculations ensured the precise timing and path necessary for the lunar module to dock with the command module in lunar orbit and for the return journey back to Earth.

Johnson's work went beyond Apollo 11. She significantly contributed to multiple space missions, including the Mercury and Gemini programs. For instance, during John Glenn's historic orbital flight aboard Friendship 7 in 1962, Johnson calculated the trajectory and coordinated the necessary data for his safe return to Earth.

Johnson's contributions shattered racial and gender barriers in the field of mathematics and science. As an African-American woman working in a predominantly white and male-dominated environment, she faced discrimination and inequality. However, her exceptional skills and undeniable talent transcended these barriers, and she gained the recognition and respect of her peers.

Johnson's remarkable achievements highlighted the importance of diversity and inclusion in scientific endeavors. Her success paved the way for future generations of women and people of color to pursue careers in STEM (science, technology, engineering, and mathematics), inspiring countless individuals to overcome societal obstacles and pursue their passions.

In 2015, Johnson's contributions were celebrated when she received the Presidential Medal of Freedom, the highest civilian honor in the United States. The following year, her story reached a broader audience with the release of the movie "Hidden Figures," which depicted the achievements of Johnson and her fellow African-American female mathematicians at NASA.

Katherine Johnson's legacy extends far beyond her individual accomplishments. Her story is a potent reminder that talent knows no boundaries and that diversity and inclusion are essential for scientific progress. Her determination, intellect, and pioneering spirit continue to inspire and motivate generations of scientists, mathematicians, and dreamers worldwide.

Radia Perlman: Inventor of Spanning Tree Protocol

Radia Perlman, born Radia Joy Green in 1951, is a highly respected computer scientist known for her significant contributions to network and protocol design. Often referred to as the "Mother of the Internet," Perlman's groundbreaking work has had a profound impact on the stability and efficiency of Ethernet networks.

One of Perlman's most notable contributions is the invention of the Spanning Tree Protocol (STP). Ethernet networks are based on a connected, loop-free topology, where data is transmitted hierarchically from one device to another. However, loops in a network can cause data to circulate endlessly, leading to network congestion and inefficiency.

Perlman recognized the need for a mechanism that would address the loop problem in Ethernet networks. In the late 1970s, she developed the Spanning Tree Protocol, a fundamental algorithm for ensuring loop-free connectivity in Ethernet networks.

The Spanning Tree Protocol works by constructing a logical tree that spans the network while identifying and disabling redundant links. This prevents data from endlessly circulating in loops and ensures only one active path between any two devices in the network. By eliminating loops, STP improves network stability, reduces congestion, and enhances the overall efficiency of Ethernet-based networks.

Perlman's Spanning Tree Protocol has become a critical component of modern networking technologies, including Ethernet-based local area networks (LANs). It is widely implemented in network switches and has been standardized as IEEE 802.1D. The protocol's effectiveness and widespread adoption have contributed to the scalability and reliability of Ethernet networks, enabling their use in large-scale enterprise networks and the internet itself.

In addition to the Spanning Tree Protocol, Perlman has made numerous other contributions to network and protocol design. She has worked on areas including network security, routing protocols, and network management. Her work has focused on improving computer network stability, efficiency, and security, and she has been granted several patents for her innovative solutions.

Perlman's expertise and contributions have been widely recognized in the field of computer networking. She has received numerous awards and accolades for her work, including being named an Internet Hall of Fame inductee in 2014. Perlman has also been a dedicated educator, sharing her knowledge and insights through teaching and mentoring.

Radia Perlman's inventions, notably the Spanning Tree Protocol, have had a lasting impact on the development and operation of computer networks. Her work has helped create a more robust and efficient networking infrastructure, facilitating the growth and connectivity of the internet and modern communication systems. Perlman's contributions continue to shape the field of computer science and inspire future generations of network engineers and protocol designers.

1.3 TRAILBLAZERS IN MATHEMATICS AND LOGIC

Emmy Noether: Revolutionizing Abstract Algebra

Emmy Noether, born Amalie Emmy Noether in 1882, was a German mathematician who made groundbreaking contributions to abstract algebra and theoretical physics. Her work significantly impacted the field of mathematics, revolutionizing our understanding of algebraic structures and their applications.

Noether's most significant contributions were ring, field, and group theories. She developed deep insights into the structure and properties of these algebraic systems, laying the foundation for modern algebra. Noether's work on rings and fields provided a rigorous framework for studying algebraic structures, including ideals, modules, and homomorphisms. Her contributions to group theory included significant advancements in the view of group actions and the concept of normal subgroups.

Noether's influence went beyond her groundbreaking work in abstract algebra. She also profoundly contributed to theoretical physics by developing Noether's theorem. This theorem, formulated in 1915, established a deep connection between symmetries and conservation laws in physics.

Noether's theorem states that there is a corresponding conserved quantity for every continuous symmetry in a physical system. In other words, the fundamental symmetries observed in nature, such as rotational symmetry or time translation symmetry, are intimately linked to the conservation of quantities like energy, momentum, and angular momentum.

This theorem had a resounding impact on theoretical physics, providing a deep understanding of the relationship between symmetries and the fundamental laws of physics. Noether's theorem is regarded as one of the most important theorems in physics and has been applied in various areas, including classical mechanics, quantum field theory, and general relativity.

Despite her groundbreaking contributions, Noether faced significant challenges in her career due to gender discrimination. She struggled to secure academic positions and often faced resistance from her male colleagues. However, her intellect and perseverance eventually led to recognition and respect within the mathematical community.

Noether's legacy is profound, as her work continues to shape mathematics and physics. Her contributions to abstract algebra and her development of Noether's theorem have had a lasting impact, providing a solid mathematical foundation for numerous areas of research and inspiring generations of mathematicians and physicists.

Emmy Noether's profound insights, perseverance in the face of adversity, and groundbreaking contributions to mathematics and physics have cemented her as one of the most influential mathematicians of the 20th century. She remains a role model for aspiring mathematicians, particularly women, and her work serves as a testament to the power of intellect and determination in pushing the boundaries of knowledge.

Hypatia of Alexandria: Scholar of Ancient Mathematics

Hypatia of Alexandria, born around 350 AD, was a remarkable mathematician who lived during a time when opportunities for women's intellectual pursuits were severely limited. Despite the societal constraints imposed on women, Hypatia made significant contributions to mathematics, leaving a lasting impact on the field.

As the head of the Neoplatonic school in Alexandria, Egypt, Hypatia's influence extended beyond mathematics and encompassed philosophy, astronomy, and other intellectual disciplines. She was known for her exceptional knowledge, eloquence, and teaching skills, attracting students and scholars from various backgrounds to study under her guidance.

In the field of algebra, Hypatia of Alexandria made significant contributions by developing methods for solving equations and simplifying mathematical expressions. While there is limited surviving documentation of her original works, historical accounts and references from her contemporaries shed light on her accomplishments in this area.

One of Hypatia's notable contributions to algebra was her work on solving linear equations. Linear equations involve unknown variables raised to the power of one and have a straightforward form, such as "$ax + b = c$." Hypatia refined existing techniques for solving such equations, demonstrating methods that helped find solutions by isolating the variable on one side of the equation.

Furthermore, Hypatia extended her work beyond linear equations and delved into more complex equations. Quadratic equations, which involve variables raised to the power of two, also received her attention. She developed techniques to solve these equations, which are crucial in physics, engineering, and other mathematical disciplines. By providing methods for finding the roots or solutions of quadratic equations, Hypatia significantly contributed to the practical applications of mathematics.

Unfortunately, Hypatia's life was tragically cut short. In 415 AD, she was brutally murdered by a mob, likely due to political and religious tensions of the time. Despite her untimely death, her legacy endured, and her contributions to mathematics and philosophy inspired scholars throughout the centuries.

Hypatia's remarkable achievements as a mathematician remain an inspiration, particularly given the societal constraints she faced. Her dedication to intellectual pursuits and her ability to excel in a male-dominated field paved the way for future generations of women in mathematics and science.

Today, Hypatia is celebrated as a symbol of resilience, intellect, and the pursuit of knowledge. Her story serves as a reminder of the importance of inclusivity and equal opportunities in education and the recognition of women's contributions to the advancement of mathematics and other fields of study.

Sophie Germain: Pioneer in Number Theory

Sophie Germain, born in 1776, was a French mathematician who made remarkable contributions to number theory and mathematical physics. Living in an era when women faced significant barriers to intellectual pursuits, Germain's determination and exceptional talent propelled her to overcome societal constraints and make groundbreaking discoveries.

Germain's work on number theory, particularly her investigations into Fermat's Last Theorem, remains a significant highlight of her contributions. Fermat's Last Theorem, proposed by Pierre de Fermat in the 17th century, stated that there are no whole number solutions to the equation $x^n + y^n = z^n$ for values of n greater than 2. Germain made significant progress in understanding the theorem and contributed to its eventual proof.

Germain's approach involved exploring the theorem by investigating cases where n is a prime number. She introduced innovative techniques, including what is now known as the "Sophie Germain prime," which is a prime number that satisfies certain conditions related to Fermat's Last Theorem. Although Germain did not fully prove Fermat's Last Theorem, her work laid the groundwork for subsequent mathematicians who eventually established the theorem in the 20th century.

In addition to number theory, Germain also made essential contributions to elasticity theory, a branch of mathematical physics concerned with the deformation and behavior of solid materials. At the time, this field was dominated by male scientists. Germain independently studied and expanded upon the work of renowned mathematician Joseph Louis Lagrange in elasticity theory, despite not having formal academic access to the subject.

Germain's research in elasticity theory earned her recognition and respect among her contemporaries, including Lagrange himself. She derived important mathematical equations that described the behavior of elastic surfaces, now known as "Germain's equations." Her work in this field paved the way for advancements in structural engineering, providing valuable insights into the mechanics of materials.

Germain's perseverance and intellectual prowess in the face of gender barriers and societal constraints established her as a respected mathematician of her time. Her contributions to number theory and mathematical physics demonstrated a deep understanding of mathematical principles and the ability to apply them in solving complex problems.

Furthermore, Germain's legacy extends beyond her specific contributions to mathematics and physics. Her accomplishments paved the way for future generations of women in mathematics, inspiring and empowering them to pursue their intellectual passions despite societal obstacles.

Part Two

Defying Expectations in Arts and Culture

2.1 FORGOTTEN ARTISTS: MASTERPIECES FROM THE SHADOWS

Artemisia Gentileschi: A Renaissance Painter Resurfaced

Artemisia Gentileschi, born in 1593, was an Italian Baroque painter who defied the gender norms and societal expectations of her time to establish herself as one of the few successful female artists of the 17th century. Despite facing personal hardships and obstacles, Gentileschi's artistic talent and emotionally charged paintings have gained increasing recognition in recent years, shedding light on her remarkable skill and distinctive perspective.

Gentileschi received her artistic training from her father, Orazio Gentileschi, who was also a painter. Under his guidance, she developed exceptional technical skills and a deep understanding of art. Her early works exhibited influences from her father and other prominent painters of the time, such as Caravaggio, known for his dramatic use of light and shadow.

However, Gentileschi's artistic journey was marked by personal struggles. At 17, she endured a traumatic event when she was sexually assaulted by Agostino Tassi, a colleague of her father. The subsequent trial, during which Gentileschi was subjected to public scrutiny and humiliation, had a lasting impact on her life and art. Despite the trauma, Gentileschi found strength and resilience in her art, channeling her emotions and experiences into her work.

Gentileschi's paintings are characterized by their powerful narratives, strong female protagonists, and an emphasis on intense emotions. She often depicted biblical and mythological scenes, infusing them with a sense of authenticity and emotional depth. Gentileschi's paintings portrayed women with agency and strength, challenging the traditional portrayal of passive female figures in art.

Her most famous works include "Judith Slaying Holofernes," a powerful and graphic depiction of the biblical heroine Judith beheading an Assyrian general, and "Susanna and the Elders," which portrays the story of Susanna confronting the harassment of two elders. In these paintings, Gentileschi explores themes of female empowerment, justice, and the female gaze, setting her apart from many of her male contemporaries.

Despite facing challenges and discrimination as a female artist, Gentileschi managed to gain recognition and success during her lifetime. She received commissions from prominent patrons, including the Medici family, and established a network of influential artists and intellectuals who admired her talent.

However, it was only in recent years that Gentileschi's exceptional skill and unique perspective gained wider appreciation and attention. Her paintings have been reevaluated and celebrated for their technical mastery, psychological depth, and contribution to the development of Baroque art.

Gentileschi's life and art have become symbols of resilience and defiance in the face of adversity. Her legacy as a pioneering female artist continues to inspire and empower women in the arts, highlighting the importance of diverse voices and perspectives in shaping the art world.

Amrita Sher-Gil: Reclaiming Identity through Art

Amrita Sher-Gil, born in 1913 to a Hungarian mother and an Indian-Sikh father, was an Indian-Hungarian painter whose artistic contributions have left an indelible mark on the art world. Sher-Gil's evocative portrayals of Indian people and culture, along with her own introspective journey of self-discovery and identity, have made her an iconic figure in the realm of modern Indian art.

Sher-Gil's artistic journey began at a young age. She displayed a natural talent for painting, and her family recognized and nurtured her creative abilities. At 16, Sher-Gil moved to Paris, where she studied at prominent art institutions, including the École des Beaux-Arts and the Grande Chaumière.

Sher-Gil was exposed to Western art movements and techniques during her time in Paris, greatly influencing her artistic style. She developed a unique blend of Western techniques with a deep-rooted connection to her Indian heritage. Her art became a visual exploration of the struggles, joys, and complexities of the Indian people and their culture.

Sher-Gil's paintings often depicted rural Indian life, particularly the lives of women, peasants, and the lower castes. She sought to capture the essence of their daily existence, their emotions, and their surroundings' vivid colors and textures. Her subjects were portrayed with honesty and empathy, reflecting India's socio-economic realities and cultural diversity.

Sher-Gil's art reflected her journey of self-discovery and identity. As a person of mixed heritage, she grappled with questions of belonging and cultural identity. Her art became a medium through which she explored and reconciled her dual heritage, bridging the gap between her Indian roots and her Western education.

Although Sher-Gil's work gained recognition posthumously, she is now celebrated as a pioneer of modern Indian art. Her paintings challenged the prevailing Eurocentric narratives of art and paved the way for a more inclusive and diverse representation of Indian culture. Sher-Gil's bold use of colors, expressive brushstrokes, and intimate portrayal of her subjects set her apart as a distinctive voice in art.

Sher-Gil's contributions extended beyond her artistry. She was a vocal advocate for the inclusion and empowerment of women artists, expressing her belief that women had a unique perspective to offer in the artistic realm. Her legacy inspires aspiring artists, particularly women, to tell their own narratives and break free from societal constraints.

Amrita Sher-Gil's artistic legacy remains a testament to the power of art to transcend boundaries and bridge cultural divides. Through her evocative and profound portrayals, she brought forth the struggles, joys, and complexities of the Indian people, leaving an enduring impact on modern Indian art and inspiring generations of artists to embrace their unique voices and cultural heritage.

Hilma af Klint: Pioneering Abstract Art

Hilma af Klint, born in 1862 in Sweden, was an artist whose visionary and abstract works predated the emergence of the abstract art movement by several years. Despite being primarily overlooked and unrecognized during her lifetime, her innovative paintings and profound exploration of mystical themes have garnered significant attention and acclaim in recent years, solidifying her status as a groundbreaking artist.

Klint's artistic journey was deeply influenced by her interest in spirituality, mysticism, and theosophy. She was part of a group of artists known as "The Five," who held séances and engaged in esoteric practices to explore spiritual realms. These experiences profoundly impacted Klint's artistic process and the themes she depicted in her work.

Klint's paintings are characterized by their abstract and geometric forms, vibrant colors, and intricate symbolism. She developed a unique visual language deeply rooted in her spiritual beliefs and desire to convey hidden truths and unseen dimensions. Her works often portrayed spiritual concepts, such as dualities, evolution, and the connection between the physical and spiritual realms.

What sets Klint apart is not only the abstract nature of her paintings but also the fact that she was creating abstract art well before it gained prominence in the art world. Her early works, dating back to 1906, predated the abstract art movement by several years, challenging the conventional timeline of art history.

During her lifetime, Klint exhibited her works in private settings and had limited public exposure. Her unconventional style and esoteric subject matter were not well understood or appreciated by the art establishment of her time. As a result, her art remained largely overlooked and unrecognized, and it was not until many years after her death that her profound contributions began to receive the attention they deserved.

In recent years, the rediscovery and reevaluation of Klint's art have led to a significant reassessment of her place in art history. Exhibitions featuring her works have attracted wide acclaim and appreciation, sparking renewed interest in her unique vision and pioneering approach to abstraction. Her groundbreaking achievements have challenged the traditional narrative of the abstract art movement and expanded our understanding of its origins.

Klint's artistic legacy extends beyond her innovative approach to abstraction. Her bold exploration of spiritual and mystical themes and her dedication to expressing unseen dimensions and hidden truths resonates with audiences today. Her work invites viewers to contemplate the intersection of art, spirituality, and the mysteries of the universe.

The recognition and celebration of Hilma af Klint's artistic genius highlight the importance of revisiting and reevaluating the contributions of overlooked artists in shaping art history. Her visionary paintings and profound exploration of abstract and mystical themes have cemented her place as a pioneering artist whose work continues to captivate and inspire audiences, offering new perspectives on the power and potential of art.

Lee Krasner: A Trailblazer of Abstract Expressionism

Born in 1908, Lee Krasner was an American abstract expressionist painter who played a pivotal role in the development of the movement, even though her contributions were often overshadowed by her husband, Jackson Pollock. Krasner's dynamic and energetic artworks showcase her mastery of color, form, and texture, challenging conventional notions of art and asserting her artistic identity.

Krasner received her formal art education at the Cooper Union and the National Academy of Design in New York City. She was exposed to various art movements and styles, including Cubism and Surrealism, which influenced her early works. However, it was during the emergence of abstract expressionism in the 1940s and 1950s that Krasner found her artistic voice.

Krasner's art is identifiable by its bold use of color, gestural brushwork, and dynamic compositions. She embraced abstraction as a means of self-expression and exploration, utilizing spontaneous and deliberate techniques to create her artworks. Krasner's canvases are often filled with vibrant and layered surfaces, reflecting her intense engagement with the creative process.

Despite her undeniable talent and contributions to the abstract expressionist movement, Krasner faced challenges in gaining recognition and establishing her artistic identity. As the wife of Jackson Pollock, who was hailed as a leading figure in abstract expressionism, Krasner was regularly overshadowed by his fame and reputation. However, she persevered and continued to create art that pushed boundaries and defied expectations.

Krasner's artistic practice was deeply rooted in her commitment to experimentation and innovation. She constantly sought new ways to challenge and expand the possibilities of abstract art. Krasner incorporated a wide range of techniques, from pouring and dripping paint to incorporating collages and elements of drawing and sculpture into her works.

Beyond her technical mastery, Krasner's art reflects her engagement with personal experiences, emotions, and cultural influences. She drew inspiration from diverse sources, including her Jewish heritage, mythology, and the natural world. Krasner's artworks often convey a sense of resilience and strength, reflecting her determination to overcome obstacles and forge her artistic path.

In later years, Krasner's art evolved and embraced a more organic and lyrical style. She explored new forms of abstraction and incorporated biomorphic shapes and rhythmic patterns into her compositions. Krasner's art continued to evolve and innovate throughout her career, demonstrating her ongoing commitment to artistic growth and exploration.

In recent years, there has been a renewed appreciation and recognition of Krasner's contributions to abstract expressionism. Major retrospectives and exhibitions have showcased her groundbreaking works, allowing audiences to fully appreciate her artistic achievements and significant role in shaping the movement.

Lee Krasner's dynamic and energetic artworks and her resilience and determination have secured her an important place in art history. Her mastery of color, form, and texture, coupled with her commitment to pushing the boundaries of abstract art, challenges the conventional notions of art and asserts her unique artistic identity. Krasner's enduring legacy reminds us of the importance of recognizing and celebrating the contributions of women artists and their invaluable impact on the art world.

Sofonisba Anguissola: Renaissance Painter of Royal Courts

Sofonisba Anguissola, born in 1532 in Cremona, Italy, was an Italian Renaissance painter who achieved remarkable recognition and success when opportunities for women in the arts were severely limited. Her skillful portraiture, characterized by a naturalistic style and psychological depth, captured the essence of her subjects and garnered her acclaim, ultimately influencing subsequent generations of artists.

Anguissola was born into a noble family that recognized and nurtured her artistic talents. Her father, Amilcare Anguissola, supported her passion for painting and ensured she received a proper artistic education. Anguissola's training began with private tutors and later extended to studying under renowned painters in Milan, including Bernardino Campi.

Anguissola's early works focused primarily on portraiture, a popular genre during the Renaissance. She developed a distinct style characterized by her attention to detail, the use of vibrant colors, and the ability to capture her subjects' individuality and inner life. Her portraits exude a sense of intimacy, often depicting her family members, friends, and herself in thoughtful and engaging compositions.

What set Anguissola apart was her ability to convey psychological depth in her portraits. She masterfully captured her subjects' emotions, expressions, and personalities, going beyond mere physical likeness. Her paintings revealed a sensitivity and understanding of human nature, making them captivating and resonant with viewers.

Anguissola's talent quickly gained recognition, and she was soon invited to the court of King Philip II of Spain, where she served as a lady-in-waiting and court painter. Her position at the Spanish court allowed her to paint portraits of noble figures, including royal family members. Her close relationship with the queen and her family further elevated her status and secured her artistic success.

Anguissola's influence extended beyond her artistic achievements. As one of the few successful female artists of her time, she became a role model for aspiring women artists. Her accomplishments challenged the prevailing gender norms and social expectations, inspiring other women to pursue their artistic passions and assert their creative voices.

Furthermore, Anguissola's influence can be seen in the work of subsequent generations of artists. One of her most famous students was the renowned painter Anthony van Dyck, who would become one of the leading portraitists of his time. Anguissola's naturalistic approach, emphasis on psychological depth, and technical skill left a lasting impact on van Dyck's artistic style.

Despite her achievements, Anguissola's contributions were overshadowed by the male-dominated art world of the time. It was not until the late 20th century that her work received the recognition it deserved. Exhibitions and scholarly research have shed light on her significant role in Renaissance art as well as her influence on subsequent generations of artists.

Sofonisba Anguissola's talent, determination, and artistic contributions have solidified her place in art history. Her ability to capture the essence of her subjects through naturalistic portraits, characterized by psychological depth, set her apart as a pioneering artist. Her achievements as a successful female artist during a time of limited opportunities continue to inspire and empower artists, particularly women, to break through barriers and assert their artistic voices.

2.2 WOMEN WRITERS: AMPLIFYING VOICES THROUGH LITERATURE

Charlotte Perkins Gilman: Challenging Gender Roles through Literature

Charlotte Perkins Gilman, an American author, feminist, and social reformer, challenged gender roles and advocated for women's rights through her literature. One of her most notable works is the groundbreaking short story "The Yellow Wallpaper," which explores the psychological and societal oppression faced by women.

"The Yellow Wallpaper," published in 1892, delves into the experiences of a woman confined to a room adorned with yellow wallpaper. The story is narrated through the woman's journal entries, revealing her descent into madness due to her confinement and the patriarchal expectations imposed upon her. Gilman's vivid descriptions and meticulous attention to the woman's mental state highlight the damaging effects of social isolation, domesticity, and the denial of self-expression.

"The Yellow Wallpaper" critiques the prevailing medical practices and societal norms that constrained women during the late 19th century. The story reflects Gilman's struggles with postpartum depression and the rest cure, a treatment prescribed for women experiencing "hysteria" or mental health issues. By exposing the detrimental consequences of such treatments, Gilman challenges the medical establishment and sheds light on the importance of empowering women to control their bodies and minds.

Gilman's advocacy for women's rights extended beyond "The Yellow Wallpaper." She was a prominent figure in the first-wave feminist movement and used her writing as a platform to address social issues and promote gender equality. In her non-fiction works, such as

"Women and Economics" (1898), Gilman examined women's economic dependence on men and argued for women's financial independence to achieve equality.

In addition to her more well-known works, Gilman also authored "Herland" (1915), a utopian novel that portrayed a society populated solely by women. The novel imagines a world free from gender inequality, where women are intellectually and physically strong and live harmoniously without the influence of patriarchy. Through "Herland," Gilman challenged traditional notions of gender roles, emphasizing the potential for a more egalitarian and inclusive society.

Gilman's writings, including "The Yellow Wallpaper" and "Herland," were instrumental in raising awareness about the oppressive structures that restricted women's autonomy and limited their opportunities for self-fulfillment. Her works provoked essential conversations about gender, mental health, and social reform, inspiring generations of feminists and serving as a catalyst for change.

While "The Yellow Wallpaper" remains Gilman's most well-known work, her broader literary contributions and advocacy for women's rights have gained increasing recognition in recent years. Her exploration of women's psychological and societal oppression continues to resonate with readers, shedding light on the enduring challenges of gender inequality and the importance of challenging traditional norms and roles.

Charlotte Perkins Gilman's courage and commitment to challenging gender roles through her literature have impacted feminist discourse and the pursuit of gender equality. Her works serve as a reminder of the power of storytelling to expose injustices, ignite social change, and empower individuals to question and challenge oppressive systems.

Zora Neale Hurston: Celebrating African-American Culture and Folklore

An influential writer and anthropologist, Zora Neale Hurston celebrated African-American culture and folklore through her acclaimed novel "Their Eyes Were Watching God" and her extensive research documenting African-Americans' rich traditions and experiences.

"Their Eyes Were Watching God," published in 1937, is considered one of Hurston's most significant literary achievements. The novel tells the story of Janie Crawford, a resilient African-American woman on a quest for self-discovery and love in the early 20th century. Through Janie's journey, Hurston explores themes of identity, gender, race, and the search for personal fulfillment within a changing society.

Hurston's novel is notable for its lyrical language, authentic dialect, and vivid portrayal of African-American life in the rural South. It delves into the complexities of African-American experiences within their communities and interactions with the broader society. By centering the story on a strong female protagonist and emphasizing the importance of personal agency, Hurston challenges traditional gender roles and celebrates the resilience and strength of African-American women.

Beyond her literary contributions, Hurston also made significant contributions as an anthropologist. She conducted extensive fieldwork, particularly in the 1930s, documenting African-American folklore, songs, dances, and oral traditions. Hurston saw the importance of preserving and celebrating these cultural expressions, which she believed were integral to the African-American identity.

Her anthropological research led her to travel throughout the southern United States and the Caribbean, collecting stories, folktales, and songs from African-American communities. Hurston's approach was unique in that she actively engaged with the individuals she studied, participating in their cultural practices and immersing herself in their communities. She recognized the importance of giving voice to the marginalized and capturing their experiences in their own words.

One of Hurston's notable works in anthropology is "Mules and Men" (1935), which chronicles her fieldwork experiences and showcases African-Americans' folklore and oral traditions in the South. In this book, Hurston presents a collection of folktales, songs, and rituals, offering readers an insight into the richness and diversity of African-

American culture.

Hurston's anthropological research and literary works were driven by a desire to challenge stereotypes and elevate the voices and experiences of African-Americans. She celebrated the cultural expressions passed down through generations and sought to highlight their significance in shaping African-American identity and community.

Although Hurston's contributions to literature and anthropology were primarily overlooked during her lifetime, her work experienced a resurgence of recognition and appreciation in the late 20th century. Her writings have become essential texts in African-American and women's studies, and her exploration of African-American culture and folklore inspires scholars and readers alike.

Zora Neale Hurston's legacy is one of celebration, preservation, and empowerment. Through her novel "Their Eyes Were Watching God" and her anthropological research, she shed light on the African-American experience, challenging stereotypes and showcasing the richness and complexity of African-American culture and traditions. Her contributions continue to be celebrated for their profound impact on literature, anthropology, and our understanding of the African-American experience.

Nella Larsen: Pioneering African-American Novelist of the Harlem Renaissance

Nella Larsen, a pioneering African-American novelist of the Harlem Renaissance, made significant contributions to the literary movement through her powerful novels, particularly "Passing" and "Quicksand." Larsen's works delve into themes of racial identity, the complexities of life for African-Americans, and the intersectionality of race, class, and gender.

Larsen's first novel, "Quicksand," published in 1928, tells the story of Helga Crane, a biracial woman struggling to find her place in a racially divided society. The novel explores Helga's journey as she navigates different worlds and grapples with the societal expectations and limitations placed upon her. Larsen skillfully depicts the challenges faced by African-Americans during the early 20th century, addressing issues of colorism, assimilation, and the quest for self-fulfillment.

In "Passing," published in 1929, Larsen delves into the concept of "passing," whereby light-skinned African-Americans choose to live as white to avoid the systemic racism and discrimination they would face otherwise. The novel centers around Irene Redfield and Clare Kendry, childhood friends who reconnect as adults. Through their complex relationship, Larsen explores themes of identity, self-deception, and the consequences of passing as white. "Passing" offers a nuanced exploration of racial ambiguity's psychological and social implications.

Larsen's novels provide a unique perspective on the experiences of African-Americans during the Harlem Renaissance, a cultural and intellectual movement that celebrated African-American art, literature, and music. While the Harlem Renaissance often emphasized a celebration of black culture and identity, Larsen's works delve into the complexities and tensions within the African-American community, challenging the notion of a monolithic black experience.

Larsen's exploration of race, class, and gender in her novels showcases her keen understanding of the intersecting forces that shape an individual's identity and experiences. She challenges societal expectations and norms, shedding light on the limitations and conflicts faced by African-Americans, particularly African-American women, in a racially stratified society.

Larsen's contributions to the Harlem Renaissance were significant, as her works provided a nuanced portrayal of African-American life and identity. While she faced challenges and criticism for her exploration of controversial themes, her novels pushed boundaries and offered a voice to the complexities and struggles faced by African-Americans.

Larsen's literary career was cut short despite the critical acclaim and recognition she initially received. She faced personal and professional challenges, including accusations of plagiarism and struggles with her identity. After publishing her second novel, Larsen largely disappeared from the literary scene and worked as a nurse.

In recent years, however, Nella Larsen's works have experienced a resurgence of interest and appreciation. Scholars and readers have recognized her novels' significance in capturing African-Americans' experiences and complexities during the Harlem Renaissance. Larsen's unique perspective and unflinching exploration of racial identity continue to resonate, making her an important figure in African-American literature.

Nella Larsen's novels, "Quicksand" and "Passing," remain powerful and relevant works that challenge societal norms and provide a nuanced understanding of the African-American experience. Her contributions to the Harlem Renaissance and her exploration of race, class, and gender continue to inspire and provoke essential conversations about identity, representation, and the complexities of human existence.

George Eliot: Challenging Gender Expectations in Victorian England

George Eliot, the pen name of Mary Ann Evans, was an influential writer of the Victorian era who challenged gender expectations through her works. Her most renowned novel, "Middlemarch," is a masterpiece of Victorian literature, exploring Victorian society's social and psychological complexities.

Published in 1871-1872, "Middlemarch" is a multi-layered novel that weaves together the lives of various characters in the fictional town of Middlemarch. Eliot meticulously delves into the intricacies of human nature, relationships, and the interplay of personal desires and societal expectations. The novel's depth and realism earned it praise as one of the greatest novels in the English language.

Through her insightful character portrayals, Eliot exposed the limitations imposed on women by Victorian society. She created complex female protagonists who challenged traditional gender roles and sought intellectual and emotional fulfillment beyond the confines of marriage and domesticity. Dorothea Brooke, one of the central characters in "Middlemarch," defies societal expectations by pursuing intellectual pursuits and marrying a man she believes shares her ideals, only to find herself disillusioned. Eliot's depiction of Dorothea's struggles reflects her critique of the limited opportunities available to women in Victorian England.

Eliot's choice to publish her works under a male pseudonym was a deliberate strategy to combat gender bias in the literary industry. By adopting the name George Eliot, she aimed to be taken seriously as a writer and avoid the prejudice faced by women in the publishing world. Despite facing initial skepticism and criticism upon revealing her true identity, Eliot ultimately gained recognition for her exceptional talent and literary contributions.

In addition to "Middlemarch," George Eliot's literary achievements encompass various novels and essays. Her other notable works include "The Mill on the Floss" (1860), which explores the conflicts between individual desires and social expectations, and "Silas Marner" (1861), a poignant tale of redemption and community. Through her writing, Eliot addressed social issues, moral dilemmas, and the complexities of human relationships, leaving a lasting impact on Victorian literature.

Eliot's portrayal of female characters challenged Victorian notions of femininity, offering a more nuanced and realistic perspective on women's lives. She emphasized her female characters' intellectual capabilities and emotional depth, presenting them as fully realized individuals with agency and aspirations beyond conventional gender roles. By doing so, Eliot paved the way for future generations of women writers and contributed to the feminist literary tradition.

George Eliot's writings not only challenged gender expectations but also delved into broader social and moral concerns. Her works explored themes such as class divisions, religious hypocrisy, and the impact of social change on individuals. Eliot's insightful observations and ability to capture the complexities of human nature continue to captivate readers and make her a significant figure in the history of literature.

Djuna Barnes: Exploring Experimental Fiction and Modernist Literature

Djuna Barnes, an American writer and artist, contributed significantly to experimental fiction and modernist literature through her groundbreaking novel "Nightwood" and her innovative narrative structure and language approach.

Published in 1936, "Nightwood" is a complex and challenging novel exploring themes of sexuality, gender identity, and unconventional relationships. Set in the bohemian nightlife of Paris and Vienna, the story follows a group of characters struggling with their desires, identities, and societal expectations. Barnes's portrayal of these characters and their relationships is deeply introspective, often delving into the depths of their emotions and inner conflicts.

One of the notable aspects of "Nightwood" is Barnes's bold and unflinching exploration of non-normative sexuality and gender. The novel depicts characters who challenge conventional sexual and gender boundaries, including Robin Vote, a woman who leaves her husband for another woman, and Dr. Matthew O'Connor, a bisexual man. Barnes's treatment of these characters and their relationships was highly unconventional for its time, offering a nuanced and sensitive portrayal of queer identities.

Barnes's experimental approach to narrative structure and language sets her apart as an innovative writer of her time. In "Nightwood," she employs a fragmented narrative style, shifting perspectives, and poetic language to create a dreamlike and introspective atmosphere. The novel's non-linear structure and unconventional use of language challenge traditional storytelling conventions and invite readers to engage with the text in a more experimental and immersive manner.

Barnes's experimentation with language is evident not only in "Nightwood" but also in her other works, such as her collection of short stories titled "A Book" (1923). In these stories, she plays with wordplay, puns, and innovative sentence structures, pushing the boundaries of literary expression and inviting readers to reconsider the limitations of language itself.

While "Nightwood" is often considered Barnes's magnum opus, her contributions to modernist literature extend beyond this novel. She actively participated in her time's avant-garde literary and artistic circles, associating with influential figures such as James Joyce, T.S. Eliot, and Ezra Pound. Her writing appeared in literary magazines and journals, showcasing her unique style and commitment to pushing traditional storytelling's boundaries.

Although Barnes's literary career was not as commercially successful as some of her contemporaries, her impact on experimental fiction and modernist literature cannot be overstated. Her bold exploration of themes, innovative narrative techniques, and commitment to challenging societal norms and conventions continue to inspire and influence writers and readers today.

2.3 MUSICIANS AND COMPOSERS: ORCHESTRATING CHANGE

Clara Schumann: Virtuoso Pianist and Composer of the Romantic Era

Clara Schumann, born Clara Wieck, was an exceptional pianist and composer of the Romantic era. Her virtuosity, musicality, and dedication to her craft made her a prominent figure in classical music.

As a pianist, Clara Schumann showcased extraordinary talent from an early age. She received rigorous training from her father, Friedrich Wieck, a renowned piano teacher. Clara's skill and musicality quickly became evident, and she embarked on a successful concert career, captivating audiences with her technical prowess and emotional depth. Her performances were praised for their precision, expressiveness, and profound interpretation of the music.

Clara's influence extended beyond her performances as she played a crucial role in shaping the development of Romantic-era music. Her collaborations with composers and musicians of the time, including her husband Robert Schumann and close friend Johannes Brahms, resulted in the exchange of ideas and artistic inspiration. Clara's insights and interpretations greatly influenced the composers, and her feedback often led to revisions and refinements in their compositions.

Clara Schumann's accomplishments as a composer are equally noteworthy. Despite the societal expectations and gender norms of the time, she composed a substantial body of work that showcased her creativity and musical genius. Her compositions encompassed various forms, including piano music, chamber music, songs, and orchestral works. Clara's compositions exhibited a deep emotional range and technical brilliance, reflecting her experiences as a performer and her unique artistic voice.

In addition to her compositions, Clara Schumann played a significant role in promoting the works of her husband, Robert Schumann. She championed his music and performed his compositions in her concerts, contributing to his recognition as one of the most influential composers of the Romantic era. Clara's dedication to her husband's musical legacy was evident even after his death, as she continued to perform and advocate for his works throughout her career.

Clara Schumann's contributions to music extended beyond her performances and compositions. She was a trailblazer for women in classical music, challenging gender norms and breaking barriers. As one of the first female concert pianists to achieve international acclaim, Clara paved the way for future generations of female musicians. Her perseverance and dedication to her art inspired many and helped reshape the perception of women's roles in music.

Billie Holiday: Transforming Jazz with Emotional Depth and Social Commentary

Billie Holiday, born Eleanora Fagan, was a legendary jazz singer-songwriter whose powerful and emotive voice revolutionized the music landscape of the 20th century. She is widely regarded as one of the greatest jazz vocalists of all time, leaving an indelible mark on the genre and influencing countless musicians.

Her unique vocal style and ability to convey raw emotions were at the heart of Billie Holiday's impact. Her voice possessed a distinct richness, depth, and expressiveness that captivated listeners. With her impeccable phrasing, nuanced delivery, and masterful control of dynamics, she breathed life into every lyric she sang. Whether performing a poignant ballad or an up-tempo swing number, Holiday had the remarkable ability to evoke a wide range of emotions in her audience, leaving them spellbound.

As a singer-songwriter, Billie Holiday left an enduring legacy. While she didn't write many of her songs, she possessed the extraordinary talent of infusing her own experiences and emotions into the music she performed. Holiday had an intuitive understanding of the nuances of a song's lyrics and melody, allowing her to interpret each piece in a deeply personal and authentic manner. Her performances were imbued with a sense of vulnerability and sincerity, making her storytelling all the more poignant.

One of Billie Holiday's most significant contributions was her courageous stance against racial injustice, mainly through her rendition of the song "Strange Fruit." Written as a poem by Abel Meeropol and set to music, "Strange Fruit" addressed the horrors of racial violence and lynching in the United States. Holiday's haunting rendition of this powerful song symbolized protest and a call for social change. By daring to perform "Strange Fruit" in the face of immense resistance and adversity, she used her platform to shed light on the injustices faced by African Americans, challenging societal norms and contributing to the Civil Rights Movement.

Beyond the impact of "Strange Fruit," Billie Holiday's entire body of work reflected her experiences and struggles as an African American woman in a racially divided society. Her songs often dealt with themes of love, heartbreak, resilience, and the complexities of human relationships. Through her performances, she navigated the highs and lows of life with remarkable authenticity and honesty, connecting with audiences on a deep emotional level.

Billie Holiday's influence extends far beyond her lifetime. Her expressive vocal style and ability to convey raw emotions continue to inspire and shape the music world. Her unique phrasing, impeccable timing, and soulful delivery influenced countless artists from various genres. Her courage in addressing social issues through her music paved the way for future musicians to use their art as a platform for change.

Fanny Mendelssohn: A Hidden Voice of Romantic Music

Fanny Mendelssohn, born Fanny Cäcilie Mendelssohn Bartholdy, was a remarkably talented composer of the Romantic era. As the older sister of renowned composer Felix Mendelssohn, Fanny possessed extraordinary musical abilities often overshadowed by her brother's success. However, her compositions, ranging from chamber music to lieder, are a testament to her musical genius and influence on the Romantic music scene.

Fanny Mendelssohn's compositions showcased her remarkable skill and depth of musical expression. Despite societal expectations discouraging women from pursuing professional music careers, Fanny defied these limitations and pursued her passion for composition. She composed over 460 works, including numerous piano pieces, chamber music, choral music, and songs.

Fanny's chamber music compositions, in particular, were highly regarded and demonstrated her exceptional talent for creating intricate and emotive musical landscapes. Her string quartets, piano trios, and piano quartets revealed her command of form, harmonic exploration, and melodic invention. Fanny's chamber music compositions were characterized by their expressive depth, captivating melodies, and masterful craftsmanship.

In addition to her chamber music, Fanny Mendelssohn excelled in composing lieder, or art songs. Her songs exhibited a deep understanding of poetry and an ability to convey its emotional essence through music. Fanny's lieder were marked by their sensitive and evocative melodies, which expertly complemented the texts she chose to set to music. Despite the limited opportunities for female composers to have their works published and performed, Fanny's songs found appreciation among her family and close friends.

Fanny's influence on the Romantic music scene extended beyond her compositions. She was crucial in fostering a vibrant musical environment within her family and social circles. Alongside Felix, Fanny hosted regular salon gatherings at the Mendelssohn family home, where prominent artists, musicians, and intellectuals would gather to discuss and perform music. These salons provided a platform for Fanny to showcase her compositions and engage in a musical exchange with fellow composers and performers.

Fanny Mendelssohn was also a significant influence on her brother

Felix. She was his confidante, collaborator, and source of inspiration. Felix often sought Fanny's advice and valued her musical opinion. Fanny's compositions profoundly impacted Felix, and her musical ideas often found their way into his works. Despite this mutual influence, societal expectations and gender norms of the time prevented Fanny from pursuing a career equal to her brother's.

It is worth noting that Fanny faced significant obstacles due to her gender. Society at the time generally discouraged women from pursuing careers as professional composers. As a result, many of Fanny's compositions were not published during her lifetime, and some were even published under Felix's name. Only recently have her works gained recognition and appreciation as independent and significant contributions to the Romantic music repertoire.

Nina Simone: Empowering Voice for Civil Rights and Musical Innovation

Nina Simone, born Eunice Kathleen Waymon, was a musician whose fusion of jazz, blues, and gospel music created a unique and powerful sound. Her exceptional voice and impassioned performances resonated with the struggles of the Civil Rights Movement, making her a significant figure in the musical and social realms of the 20th century.

Simone's musical style defied categorization, seamlessly blending jazz, blues, gospel, soul, and classical music elements. Drawing from her classical piano training, she infused her performances with intricate melodies, expressive phrasing, and rich harmonies. Her soulful and emotionally charged voice brought depth and authenticity to her music, captivating audiences and establishing her as a vocal powerhouse.

Nina Simone's role as an activist was inseparable from her music. She used her platform to address social and racial inequality, becoming an influential voice in the fight for civil rights. Through her songs, she confronted the realities of discrimination and expressed the pain and frustration of marginalized communities.

One of Simone's most iconic songs, "To Be Young, Gifted and Black," became an anthem for the Civil Rights Movement. Inspired by a play of the same name by Lorraine Hansberry, the song celebrated black identity and encouraged empowerment and self-acceptance. Its lyrics conveyed a message of pride, resilience, and hope, resonating deeply with African Americans and serving as a rallying cry for equality.

Simone's activism extended beyond her music. She actively participated in civil rights demonstrations and used her concerts as platforms to speak out against racial injustice. Her performances often included politically charged statements, and she unapologetically addressed race, inequality, and social justice issues.

Simone's unwavering commitment to activism led to her being labeled the "High Priestess of Soul" and earned her respect as a prominent figure in the civil rights movement. She performed at influential events such as the Selma to Montgomery marches and used her talent and influence to shed light on the struggles faced by African Americans. Her song choices, such as "Mississippi Goddam," a scathing critique of racial violence and segregation, exemplified her unflinching dedication to challenging the status quo.

Simone's music and activism were intertwined, with her powerful voice serving as a vessel for social commentary and protest. Through her artistry, she sought to inspire change, ignite conversations, and amplify the voices of the oppressed. Her music continues to resonate with audiences today, reminding us of the ongoing struggle for equality and the power of music as a catalyst for social change.

Part Three

Unsung Leaders and Change-makers

3.1 VISIONARIES OF SOCIAL JUSTICE MOVEMENTS

Rosa Parks: The Mother of the Civil Rights Movement

Rosa Parks, an African-American civil rights activist, is best known for her pivotal role in the Montgomery Bus Boycott, a landmark event in the Civil Rights Movement. On December 1, 1955, in Montgomery, Alabama, Parks refused to give up her bus seat to a white passenger, defying the segregation laws of the time. This act of defiance sparked a wave of protests, leading to the Montgomery Bus Boycott, a 381-day campaign that eventually led to the desegregation of public transportation in the city.

Parks' refusal to relinquish her seat on that fateful day was not a spur-of-the-moment act but a deliberate and calculated stand against racial inequality. As an active member of the local chapter of the National Association for the Advancement of Colored People (NAACP), Parks had long been involved in the fight against racial segregation. Her act of resistance on the bus culminated in her experiences with discrimination and her commitment to seeking justice and equality.

The Montgomery Bus Boycott, which began after Parks' arrest, marked a turning point in the Civil Rights Movement. The boycott saw African-Americans in Montgomery refusing to use the city's buses, instead organizing carpools, walking, or using alternative means of transportation. The boycott was a remarkable display of unity, determination, and peaceful protest, with Parks at the forefront as a symbol of resistance and a catalyst for change.

Parks' actions and the subsequent boycott garnered national attention and support, highlighting the systemic racism and injustice embedded in American society. The embargo challenged discriminatory public transportation practices and galvanized a broader movement against racial segregation and discrimination.

Parks remained committed to activism and fighting for civil rights throughout her life. She continued her work with the NAACP, advocating for racial equality, voter registration, and social justice. Parks' contributions extended beyond the Montgomery Bus Boycott, as she became an iconic figure in the struggle for civil rights in the United States.

Parks' courageous act and tireless activism inspired and influenced a generation of activists, providing a spark of hope and determination to fight against racial injustice. Her legacy transcends that single act of defiance, as she became an emblem of resistance and a symbol of the power of ordinary individuals to effect meaningful change.

Rosa Parks' steadfast commitment to justice, equality, and nonviolent resistance has left an indelible mark on history. Her bravery and refusal to accept the status quo ignited a movement that challenged segregation and paved the way for future civil rights victories. Rosa Parks remains an icon of the Civil Rights Movement, reminding us of the power of individual actions and the importance of standing up against injustice. Her unwavering dedication to the cause of racial equality continues to inspire generations and serves as a potent reminder that one person's defiance can spark a movement and change the course of history.

Malala Yousafzai: Champion of Education and Girls' Rights

Malala Yousafzai, a Pakistani activist, is widely recognized for her fearless advocacy for girls' education in Pakistan and beyond. Born on July 12, 1997, in the Swat Valley region of Pakistan, Malala grew up in an environment where the Taliban's influence was steadily growing, and girls' access to education was increasingly restricted.

From a young age, Malala recognized the power of education and the importance of girls' empowerment. Inspired by her father, who also advocated for education, Malala began speaking out about the right to education for all, particularly girls, through her anonymous blog on

BBC Urdu. She gained international recognition when she was 11 years old, highlighting girls' challenges in accessing education under Taliban rule.

However, in 2012, at the age of 15, Malala's activism took a terrifying turn when the Taliban targeted her. On her way home from school, a masked gunman boarded her school bus and shot her in the head. The assassination attempt shocked the world and brought international attention to the plight of girls seeking an education in areas controlled by extremists.

Miraculously, Malala survived the attack and underwent extensive medical treatment and rehabilitation in the United Kingdom. Her determination to continue her advocacy only grew stronger. She became a symbol of resilience and defiance against oppression, using her voice and platform to advocate for the rights of girls and women globally.

Malala's remarkable journey led to numerous accolades and recognition for her activism. In 2013, she delivered a powerful speech at the United Nations, calling for universal access to education. The same year, she co-authored her memoir, "I Am Malala," sharing her story with the world and further inspiring others to stand up for the right to education.

In 2014, at 17, Malala became the youngest-ever Nobel Prize laureate when she was awarded the Nobel Peace Prize for her courageous and determined efforts to advocate for girls' education. This prestigious honor solidified her status as a global symbol of hope and a leader in the fight for educational rights.

Since then, Malala has continued championing girls' education through the Malala Fund, which she co-founded with her father. The Malala Fund empowers girls and ensures their access to quality education in vulnerable communities. Malala has traveled to different parts of the world, including refugee camps, to highlight education's importance and amplify the voices of marginalized girls and women.

Dolores Huerta: Advocate for Farmworkers' Rights and Latinx Empowerment

Dolores Huerta, an American labor leader and civil rights activist, has played a pivotal role in advocating for farmworkers' rights and fighting for social and economic justice. Born on April 10, 1930, in New Mexico, Huerta witnessed the hardships faced by farmworkers and experienced the injustices of inequality firsthand.

Huerta co-founded the United Farm Workers (UFW) union alongside Cesar Chavez in 1962. Together, they fought for fair wages, better working conditions, and the empowerment of farmworkers, who were predominantly Latinx and faced exploitation and discrimination. Huerta's tireless efforts as a labor leader were instrumental in mobilizing farmworkers and raising awareness about their struggles.

One of the defining moments in Huerta's activism was the successful Delano grape strike in 1965, where the UFW, under her leadership, organized a boycott against table grape growers to demand fair treatment for farmworkers. The campaign garnered significant support across the country, drawing attention to the plight of farmworkers and pressuring growers to negotiate better labor contracts.

Huerta's activism extended beyond labor rights and encompassed broader social and political issues. She emphasized the importance of intersectionality, recognizing the interconnectedness of various struggles related to race, gender, and immigration. Huerta actively advocated for the rights of Latinx communities and fought against systemic oppression.

Her commitment to social and economic justice led her to engage in political activism and community organizing. She co-founded the Political Association of Spanish-Speaking Organizations (PASO) and worked to register Latinx voters, empowering them to have a voice in the political process.

Huerta's activism for Latinx communities also included advocating for bilingual education, access to healthcare, and immigrant rights. She recognized the need for systemic change and worked to dismantle structures that perpetuated inequality and discrimination.

Huerta faced numerous challenges throughout her career, including violence, arrests, and personal attacks. However, her unwavering dedication to the cause and her ability to mobilize people through nonviolent means were crucial to her advocacy success.

Huerta's contributions and legacy as a social justice leader have been widely recognized. She has received numerous awards, including the Presidential Medal of Freedom, and continues to inspire and empower others through her activism and advocacy. At 91, she remains actively involved in grassroots organizing and continues fighting for marginalized communities' rights and dignity.

Dolores Huerta's work as a United Farm Workers union co-founder and lifelong commitment to social and economic justice have left an indelible mark on American history. Her tireless efforts have improved the lives of countless farmworkers, uplifted Latinx communities, and inspired generations of activists to fight for equality and justice.

Audre Lorde: Intersectional Feminist and Literary Trailblazer

Audre Lorde, an influential writer, poet, and activist, significantly contributed to feminist and social justice movements through her powerful and thought-provoking work. Born on February 18, 1934, in New York City, Lorde dedicated her life to challenging power systems, exploring intersectional feminism, and advocating for the rights of marginalized communities.

Lorde's writings encompassed a range of genres, including poetry, essays, and memoirs. Her poetry collections, such as "The Black Unicorn" and "Coal," are known for their lyrical intensity and how they address themes of identity, race, sexuality, and social inequality. Lorde's poetry often offered a profound exploration of personal experiences while shedding light on broader social and political issues.

In addition to her poetry, Lorde's essays were instrumental in shaping feminist theory and activism. Her collection of essays titled "Sister Outsider" is particularly renowned for examining the intersections of race, gender, and sexuality. In these essays, Lorde critiqued the limitations of mainstream feminism, emphasizing the importance of intersectionality and the need to address the unique struggles faced by marginalized groups, particularly Black women.

Lorde's concept of intersectionality, which recognizes that individuals experience overlapping forms of oppression and privilege, challenged the dominant feminist discourse of her time. She argued that true liberation could only be achieved by dismantling the interconnected systems of oppression that marginalized and silenced certain groups within society.

Furthermore, Lorde's writings often centered on the experiences of Black women and other marginalized individuals. She explored the complexities of identity, the power dynamics inherent in systems of oppression, and the need for solidarity among marginalized communities. Lorde emphasized the importance of recognizing and embracing differences, rejecting the notion of a single, monolithic feminist movement.

Beyond her literary contributions, Lorde was an outspoken activist, actively engaging in various social justice causes. She was deeply involved in the civil rights movement, feminist movements, and LGBTQ+ rights advocacy. Lorde consistently used her platform to amplify the voices of those who were marginalized and to challenge systemic inequalities.

Lorde's advocacy work and writings aimed to empower individuals to embrace their identities, resist oppression, and strive for social change. She encouraged people to speak their truths and recognize their voices' power.

Wangari Maathai: Environmentalist and Women's Rights Advocate

Wangari Maathai, a renowned Kenyan environmentalist, activist, and

Nobel laureate, made groundbreaking contributions to sustainable development, democracy, and women's empowerment in Kenya and beyond. Born on April 1, 1940, in Nyeri, Kenya, Maathai's work as the founder of the Green Belt Movement revolutionized environmental conservation efforts. It brought attention to the intersectionality of ecological, social, and political issues.

Maathai's most notable achievement was the establishment of the Green Belt Movement in 1977. The organization's primary goal was to address deforestation, soil erosion, and environmental degradation in Kenya. Maathai initiated a tree-planting campaign through the movement, mobilizing women in rural communities to plant trees to combat deforestation and improve land and water resources. The movement contributed to environmental conservation and aimed to empower women by providing income-generating opportunities and promoting their active participation in decision-making.

Maathai recognized the connection between environmental degradation, poverty, and the marginalization of women. By involving women in environmental activism and sustainable development projects, she challenged traditional gender roles and empowered women to become agents of change within their communities. The Green Belt Movement's approach effectively combined environmental conservation with women's empowerment, promoting a holistic and sustainable approach to development.

Beyond her work in environmental conservation, Maathai was a prominent advocate for democracy, human rights, and social justice in Kenya. She spoke out against political corruption, land grabbing, and social inequalities, often facing opposition and persecution from the government. Her activism was deeply rooted in the belief that environmental sustainability is closely linked to good governance and the protection of human rights.

In recognition of her outstanding efforts, Maathai became the first African woman to receive the Nobel Peace Prize in 2004. The award acknowledged her significant contributions to promoting sustainable development, democracy, and peace. The Nobel committee highlighted her work in combining environmental conservation, social justice, and women's empowerment, recognizing the interconnectedness of these issues and their impact on peace and stability.

Maathai's legacy extends far beyond her work in Kenya. Her influential voice and activism inspired individuals and organizations worldwide to take action for the environment and social justice. She demonstrated that grassroots movements led by empowered women could make a significant difference in addressing environmental challenges and promoting sustainable development.

Wangari Maathai's groundbreaking work inspires generations of environmentalists, activists, and advocates for social change. Her legacy reminds us of the importance of addressing environmental issues through an inclusive and gender-responsive approach, recognizing the interconnectedness of ecological sustainability, human rights, and democratic governance. Through her courage, determination, and commitment to a better future, Maathai left an indelible mark on the global movement for environmental conservation, women's empowerment, and sustainable development.

3.2 WOMEN WARRIORS: CHALLENGING GENDER NORMS

Nakano Takeko: Fearless Samurai Warrior of Feudal Japan

Nakano Takeko, a remarkable female samurai warrior, lived during the Edo period in Japan (1603-1868) and left a lasting legacy through her exceptional martial arts skills, leadership abilities, and unwavering commitment to defending her clan and ideals. Despite living in a society that often restricted the role of women in warfare, Takeko defied conventions and became a symbol of strength and bravery.

Born in 1847 in the Aizu domain (present-day Fukushima Prefecture), Takeko was raised in a martial arts family and received rigorous training from an early age. She excelled in various combat techniques, including using the naginata, a polearm weapon traditionally associated with samurai women. Takeko's mastery of the naginata made her a formidable warrior and leader on the battlefield.

Takeko's skills were tested during the turbulent Boshin War (1868-1869), a conflict between forces supporting the imperial government and those loyal to the Tokugawa shogunate. The Aizu domain aligned with the shogunate, and Takeko joined the Women's Army Corps, a group of women who fought alongside the male samurai. The corps was established to defend Aizu Castle, the stronghold of the Aizu domain.

During the Battle of Aizu in 1868, Takeko displayed exceptional leadership and strategic prowess. Leading a contingent of female warriors, she fought fiercely against the imperial forces. Takeko's battlefield achievements and charismatic presence inspired her comrades and struck fear into the hearts of their enemies. It is said that Takeko personally took down several opponents before being fatally shot in the chest.

Knowing her death was imminent, Takeko made a final request to her sister, asking her to remove her head to prevent the enemy from mutilating her body. According to some accounts, Takeko wrote a death poem with her blood on a piece of cloth, emphasizing her loyalty to her clan and her willingness to sacrifice her life for their cause.

Although Takeko's life was cut short at age 21, her legacy as a female samurai warrior endures. Her unwavering commitment to her clan, exceptional martial arts skills, and leadership during battles have made her a revered figure in Japanese history. Takeko's story challenges traditional gender roles and highlights women's significant contributions on the battlefield, despite societal restrictions.

In recent years, Nakano Takeko has been celebrated as a symbol of female empowerment and a source of inspiration for women in Japan and worldwide. Her story serves as a reminder of the courage, strength, and determination individuals can demonstrate in the face of adversity. Takeko's unwavering spirit continues to resonate, reminding us of the importance of pursuing our beliefs and standing up for what we hold dear, regardless of societal expectations or limitations.

Queen Tamar: Fierce Ruler and Military Strategist of Georgia

Queen Tamar, a powerful ruler of medieval Georgia, left a lasting legacy through her exceptional leadership, military prowess, and diplomatic skills. As one of Georgia's most revered monarchs, she played a crucial role in expanding the kingdom's influence and ensuring its stability during a turbulent era.

Born in 1160, Tamar ascended to the throne in 1184 at 24 following her father's death, King George III. Queen Tamar demonstrated remarkable intelligence, determination, and a strong sense of duty towards her kingdom from the beginning of her reign. She was determined to continue the policies of her predecessors and further strengthen Georgia's position in the region.

One of Queen Tamar's most notable achievements was her military leadership. She was not merely a figurehead ruler but actively participated in military campaigns, leading her armies into battle. Under her command, Georgia experienced a series of military successes, expanding its territories and establishing control over various regions. Queen Tamar's military victories included campaigns against neighboring powers such as the Seljuk Turks, the Khwarazmian Empire, and the Byzantine Empire.

Beyond her military achievements, Queen Tamar was a skilled diplomat and strategist. She recognized the importance of forging alliances and maintaining diplomatic relations with neighboring states. Through her shrewd diplomacy, Tamar established beneficial alliances with powerful rulers such as the Byzantine Emperor and the Shah of Khwarazm. These alliances ensured Georgia's security and facilitated cultural and economic exchanges, contributing to the kingdom's growth and prosperity.

Queen Tamar's reign was characterized by a strong focus on domestic governance and promoting justice and religious tolerance. She enacted legal reforms and established a fair and efficient judicial system. Tamar actively supported the Georgian Orthodox Church and its clergy, strengthening her popular support and the kingdom's unity.

Queen Tamar's reign is often called the "Golden Age" of Georgia. Her accomplishments profoundly impacted Georgian culture, arts, and architecture development. Numerous churches and monasteries were built during her rule, showcasing a unique blend of Georgian, Byzantine, and Persian architectural styles.

Tamar's legacy extends beyond her lifetime. She is celebrated as a national hero, symbolizing Georgian unity, strength, and resilience. Her reign marked a period of stability, expansion, and cultural flourishing for Georgia. Queen Tamar's leadership and accomplishments continue to inspire Georgians and serve as a testament to the power and influence of women in positions of authority.

Nanny of the Maroons: Revolutionary Fighter for Jamaican Freedom

Nanny, also known as Queen Nanny or Granny Nanny, was a remarkable leader and military strategist who played a pivotal role in the resistance against British colonial forces in Jamaica during the 18th century. As a prominent figure among the Maroons, a community of escaped enslaved Africans, Nanny's tactical brilliance and unwavering determination symbolized resistance and liberation.

Nanny was born in West Africa, most likely in present-day Ghana, and was brought to Jamaica as an enslaved person during the transatlantic slave trade. She belonged to the Ashanti tribe, known for their strong warrior traditions and resistance against enslavement. Drawing on her African heritage and experiences as an enslaved person, Nanny became a central figure in organizing and leading the Maroon resistance.

Nanny's leadership abilities and military strategies were instrumental in the Maroons' successful resistance against the British forces. She utilized guerrilla warfare tactics, employing hit-and-run techniques and utilizing the rugged terrain of the Jamaican mountains to her advantage. Nanny's knowledge of the land and understanding of the British military tactics allowed her to outmaneuver and ambush the colonial troops.

Under Nanny's guidance, the Maroons established a network of communities in the mountainous regions of Jamaica, creating independent enclaves where escaped enslaved people could find refuge and live freely. These communities became known as Maroon towns, and Nanny's influence extended beyond her immediate followers. She was respected and revered within her community and among other Maroon groups and enslaved populations who looked to her as a source of inspiration and leadership.

Nanny's legacy as a freedom fighter and liberator continues to be celebrated in Jamaica and the wider African diaspora. She is revered as a symbol of resistance, courage, and perseverance. Her determination to defy the oppressive system of slavery and fight for the freedom of her people has earned her a prominent place in Jamaican history and the pantheon of African diasporic heroes.

While Nanny's exact life details and accomplishments may be shrouded in some historical ambiguity, her impact on the struggle for freedom and establishing independent Maroon communities is widely recognized. Her ability to unite her people, her strategic brilliance in combat, and her unwavering commitment to resistance serve as a testament to her remarkable life and the enduring legacy of her leadership.

Today, Nanny is celebrated as a national hero in Jamaica, with her image appearing on the country's banknotes, and her legacy is honored through various memorials, including the Nanny Town Heritage Route, which allows visitors to trace her footsteps and learn about her courageous life. Nanny's story is a testament to the indomitable spirit of those who fought for freedom and justice, impacting the quest for human dignity and equality.

Khutulun: Mongolian Wrestler Princess and Military Strategist

Khutulun, also known as Aigiarne or Aiyurug, was a remarkable Mongolian warrior princess who lived during the 13th and 14th centuries. She was the daughter of Kaidu Khan, a prominent Mongol ruler and a descendant of Genghis Khan. Khutulun's prowess in wrestling, her military acumen, and her fearless nature set her apart as an exceptional figure in Mongolian history.

Khutulun grew up in a nomadic society that valued physical strength, martial skills, and military leadership. From a young age, she displayed a natural talent for wrestling and combat, excelling in skill and strength. It is said that she was undefeated in numerous wrestling matches and that she possessed a rare combination of agility, technique, and power. Her wrestling prowess became a source of pride for her father and tribe.

In addition to her wrestling abilities, Khutulun actively participated in military campaigns alongside her father. She proved herself a skilled strategist and warrior, demonstrating her military acumen and leadership capabilities on the battlefield. Khutulun's presence and contributions in battles were highly regarded, and she gained a reputation as a fierce and fearless warrior.

Khutulun's reputation as an unbeatable wrestler and her military achievements brought honor to herself and her tribe. According to historical accounts, Khutulun challenged potential suitors, stating that any man who wanted to marry her must defeat her in wrestling and offer her horses as a bet. Legend has it that she defeated countless suitors, amassing a substantial herd of horses in the process.

Khutulun's story has been preserved through historical records and oral traditions, and her remarkable feats have become a source of inspiration and admiration. Her strength, skill, and bravery challenged gender norms and defied expectations, earning her a prominent place in Mongolian folklore and history.

While details of Khutulun's life may be subject to interpretation and legend, her significance as a warrior princess and her cultural impact cannot be denied. Her story is a testament to the strength and capabilities of women in Mongolian society, and she is celebrated as a symbol of female empowerment and resilience.

Today, Khutulun's legacy continues to be celebrated in Mongolia and beyond. She represents the spirit of independence, strength, and fearlessness, inspiring others to break barriers and pursue their ambitions. Khutulun's remarkable wrestling skills and military achievements have left an indelible mark on Mongolian history, ensuring her place as a legendary figure in the annals of warrior princesses.

Lakshmi Bai: The Rani of Jhansi and Symbol of Indian Resistance

Lakshmi Bai, popularly known as the Rani of Jhansi, was a fearless leader pivotal in the Indian Rebellion of 1857, also known as the Indian Mutiny or the First War of Independence. Born in 1828 in Varanasi, India, she was named Manikarnika Tambe at birth and later adopted the name Lakshmi Bai upon her marriage to Raja Gangadhar Rao, the ruler of Jhansi.

Lakshmi Bai's leadership qualities and commitment to the cause of Indian independence became evident after the death of her husband in 1853, which left her as the regent of Jhansi and the guardian of her adopted son. When the Indian Rebellion erupted in 1857, Lakshmi Bai refused to surrender her kingdom to the British and took a bold stand against their oppressive rule.

Under her leadership, Lakshmi Bai became an emblem of resistance and resilience. She organized and trained a force of both men and women to defend Jhansi against the British. Despite being outnumbered and facing superior weaponry, Lakshmi Bai's military strategies and bravery on the battlefield became legendary. She fought alongside her troops, inspiring them with her courage and determination.

During the siege of Jhansi, Lakshmi Bai's forces held out against the British for several weeks before eventually being forced to retreat. Undeterred by the loss, she continued to lead her troops in guerilla warfare and launched a successful counterattack, reclaiming Jhansi for a brief period. However, her efforts to secure her kingdom and independence were ultimately challenged by the overwhelming British forces.

In June 1858, Lakshmi Bai and her forces faced a decisive battle at Gwalior. Despite a valiant fight, the outnumbered Indian rebels were overwhelmed, and Lakshmi Bai was forced to flee the battlefield. Tragically, she lost her life during the battle, becoming a martyr for the cause of Indian independence.

Lakshmi Bai's legacy as a brave warrior and a symbol of resistance remains strong. Her unwavering determination, leadership skills, and commitment to her people have made her an enduring figure in Indian history. She is remembered as a fierce and courageous queen who defied gender norms and fought alongside her troops on the frontlines.

Lakshmi Bai's role in the Indian Rebellion 1857 and her unwavering dedication to the cause of Indian independence continue to inspire generations. Her story has been immortalized in literature, poetry, and folklore, and she is celebrated as a national hero in India. Lakshmi Bai's contributions to the fight against colonial rule and her steadfast spirit in the face of adversity have left an indelible mark on the collective memory of the Indian people.

3.3 TRAILBLAZING POLITICIANS AND DIPLOMATS

Sirimavo Bandaranaike: World's First Female Prime Minister

Sirimavo Bandaranaike, the world's first female prime minister, pioneered Sri Lankan and global politics. Born on April 17, 1916, in the small town of Ratnapura, Sri Lanka, she entered the political arena following the assassination of her husband, Solomon Bandaranaike, who served as the country's prime minister.

In 1960, Sirimavo Bandaranaike led the Sri Lanka Freedom Party (SLFP) to victory in the general elections, becoming the first woman in the world to hold the position of prime minister. Her election marked a significant milestone for gender equality in politics and opened doors for women in leadership roles worldwide.

As prime minister, Bandaranaike implemented a range of social and economic reforms. She prioritized education, introduced policies to increase access to schooling, particularly for girls, and expanded healthcare services. Land reforms aimed at redistributing land to farmers and empowering rural communities were also implemented under her leadership.

Furthermore, Bandaranaike played a prominent role in international politics, particularly in the Non-Aligned Movement (NAM). As the leader of Sri Lanka, she actively supported the principles of non-alignment and advocated for the rights of developing nations. Bandaranaike's contributions to the NAM helped shape its agenda and promote global cooperation and solidarity.

Regarding gender equality, Bandaranaike's tenure had a lasting impact on women's rights and political representation. She championed policies to empower women and promote their participation in public life. Bandaranaike encouraged women's involvement in decision-making and appointed several women to key government positions, breaking barriers and inspiring future generations of female leaders.

Bandaranaike's political career faced its share of challenges and controversies. Her second term as prime minister began in 1970 and was marked by political instability and economic difficulties. However, her influence as a trailblazing leader and her commitment to social justice and equality continued to resonate.

After serving three terms as prime minister, Sirimavo Bandaranaike remained influential in Sri Lankan politics. She held various government positions and advocated for women's rights and social welfare until her retirement in 2000.

Sirimavo Bandaranaike's historic achievement as the world's first female prime minister, her policy reforms, and her contributions to the Non-Aligned Movement have left an indelible mark on Sri Lanka's political landscape and the global fight for gender equality. Her legacy as a trailblazer and her efforts to empower women and marginalized communities continue to inspire and shape political discourse today.

Jeannette Rankin: First Woman Elected to the United States Congress

Jeannette Rankin's historic achievement as the first woman elected to the United States Congress in 1916 marked a significant milestone for women's representation in American politics. Born on June 11, 1880, in Missoula, Montana, Rankin was a trailblazer who paved the way for future generations of women in government.

Rankin's entry into politics was driven by her passion for social justice and commitment to advocating for the rights of women and marginalized communities. As a suffragist, she played a vital role in the women's suffrage movement, actively campaigning for women's right to vote. Her tireless efforts contributed to the passing of the 19th Amendment in 1920, which granted women the right to vote in the

United States.

During her time in Congress, Rankin's advocacy for peace was a defining characteristic of her political career. She staunchly opposed war and was known for her pacifist beliefs, gaining national attention for her courageous vote against the United States' entry into World War I in 1917. Rankin firmly believed in diplomacy and peaceful resolutions to conflicts and dedicated herself to promoting peaceful solutions in international affairs.

Beyond her pacifist stance, Rankin was a champion for social justice and equality. She fought for labor rights, supported legislation to protect women and children, and advocated for social welfare programs. Rankin consistently used her platform to amplify the voices of the marginalized and worked to address the systemic inequalities present in American society.

Rankin's political career faced challenges and obstacles, particularly as a woman in a predominantly male-dominated political landscape. However, her resilience and determination paved the way for future women leaders in the United States. Her commitment to progressive causes and her unwavering dedication to social justice made her a symbol of hope and inspiration for many.

Although Rankin's tenure in Congress was relatively short—she served two non-consecutive terms, first from 1917 to 1919 and again from 1941 to 1943—her impact was long-lasting. Her historic achievement as the first woman in Congress broke barriers and shattered gender norms, opening doors for women to participate in politics.

Jeannette Rankin's legacy as a pioneering advocate for peace, women's suffrage, and social justice continues to inspire generations of activists and leaders. Her determination to challenge the status quo and her unwavering commitment to equality serves as a reminder of the power of individuals to effect meaningful change. Rankin's historic achievement and lifelong dedication to progressive causes remain integral to the ongoing fight for gender equality and social justice in the United States.

Madeleine Albright: Diplomatic Trailblazer and First Female U.S. Secretary of State

Her remarkable achievements mark Madeleine Albright's career as the first female U.S. Secretary of State and her significant contributions to diplomacy and international relations. Born on May 15, 1937, in Prague, Czechoslovakia (now the Czech Republic), Albright's journey to becoming a trailblazing diplomat is a testament to her intelligence, resilience, and commitment to public service.

Albright's tenure as Secretary of State under President Bill Clinton from 1997 to 2001 was groundbreaking. She shattered the glass ceiling and paved the way for women in high-level positions of power and influence in the United States government. Her appointment symbolized progress and represented a significant step toward gender equality in American politics.

As Secretary of State, Albright played a pivotal role in shaping U.S. foreign policy and navigating complex international challenges. She was known for her diplomatic acumen, strong leadership, and ability to engage in constructive dialogue with world leaders. Albright worked tirelessly to promote democracy, human rights, and stability on the global stage.

Albright's diplomatic achievements were numerous and impactful. She was crucial in negotiating and implementing the Dayton Accords, which ended the war in Bosnia and Herzegovina. Her efforts to broker peace and promote reconciliation in the Balkans were instrumental in restoring stability to the region.

Additionally, Albright strengthened diplomatic ties with countries such as China, Russia, and North Korea. She engaged in diplomatic efforts to address nuclear proliferation, including negotiations with North Korea over its nuclear program. Albright's engagement with world leaders and her commitment to diplomatic solutions exemplified her dedication to maintaining global peace and security.

Beyond her diplomatic achievements, Albright was a vocal advocate for democracy, human rights, and women's empowerment. She emphasized the importance of democratic governance and consistently pushed for the expansion of democratic principles worldwide. Albright believed in the power of diplomacy and dialogue to address conflicts and promote positive change.

Albright's leadership extended beyond her role as Secretary of State. After leaving office, she continued to be an influential voice in international affairs, writing books, delivering lectures, and participating in public debates on global issues. She founded the Albright Stonebridge Group, a global strategy firm, and remains influential in international relations.

Golda Meir: Iron Lady and Israel's First Female Prime Minister

Golda Meir, born on May 3, 1898, in Kyiv, Russian Empire (now Ukraine), left an enduring political legacy as Israel's first female prime minister and one of the most influential leaders in Israeli history. Her remarkable leadership during challenging times, commitment to social justice, and efforts to strengthen Israel's international relations have made her a highly respected figure in Israel and globally.

Golda Meir's political career began in the early years of Israel's statehood. She played a pivotal role in the country's establishment and served in various leadership positions before assuming the role of prime minister. Meir's political ideology was rooted in socialist Zionism, emphasizing the importance of a strong and independent Jewish state.

As prime minister from 1969 to 1974, Meir faced significant challenges, including regional conflicts, economic crises, and diplomatic pressures. Her leadership during the Yom Kippur War of 1973 demonstrated her resilience and determination to protect and defend Israel. Despite initial setbacks, she successfully led Israel through the war, ensuring the country's survival and restoring a sense of security.

Meir's contributions to Israel's international relations were substantial. She focused on building diplomatic alliances, particularly with the

United States, to secure support for Israel's security and legitimacy. Meir played a significant role in strengthening ties between Israel and other countries, forging diplomatic relationships that continue to shape Israel's foreign policy today.

Meir's commitment to social justice and equality was central to her political agenda. She believed in equal rights for all citizens, regardless of background or ethnicity. Meir advocated for gender equality and worked to empower women in Israeli society, promoting their participation in politics and decision-making processes. Her tenure as prime minister marked a significant milestone for women's rights and representation in Israeli politics.

Meir's dedication to social justice went further than gender equality. She prioritized the welfare of Israeli citizens, striving to improve living conditions, access to education, and healthcare. Meir believed in the importance of social and economic development to foster a stable and cohesive society.

Golda Meir's political legacy transcends her time in office. Her leadership and determination have made her an enduring symbol of Israeli resilience and strength. Meir's commitment to social justice, equality, and the pursuit of peace inspires leaders worldwide. Her contributions to Israel's international relations and shaping Israeli society have left an indelible mark on the country's history and path forward.

Vigdís Finnbogadóttir: Pioneering President and Global Advocate for Women

Vigdís Finnbogadóttir, born on April 15, 1930, in Reykjavík, Iceland, is the world's first democratically elected female president. Her transformative presidency, advocacy for cultural preservation, and impact on gender equality and women's empowerment have made her an influential figure in Icelandic politics and a global inspiration.

Finnbogadóttir's presidency spanned an impressive period of 16 years, from 1980 to 1996. During her time in office, she focused on building a strong and inclusive Iceland, promoting national identity, and fostering cultural preservation. She became a symbol of national unity and pride, leveraging her role as president to elevate Icelandic arts, literature, and cultural heritage.

One of Finnbogadóttir's notable contributions was her emphasis on the importance of cultural preservation and promotion. She recognized that culture and the arts are integral to a nation's identity and worked tirelessly to support Icelandic artists and creators. Under her leadership, the importance of cultural heritage and artistic expression was elevated domestically and internationally.

Finnbogadóttir's impact on gender equality and women's empowerment continues today. As the world's first democratically elected female president, she shattered gender barriers and became a trailblazer for women in politics. Her election inspired women across the globe, proving that women can attain the highest positions of political power.

Throughout her presidency, Finnbogadóttir actively promoted women's rights and worked towards creating a more inclusive society. She established the Women's Alliance to advance gender equality and improve women's representation in Icelandic politics. Under her leadership, Iceland made significant strides in achieving gender parity and became a global leader in women's empowerment.

Finnbogadóttir's presidency coincided with a period of social and political change in Iceland. She was crucial in shaping the country's transition towards a more modern and egalitarian society. Her leadership style, characterized by warmth, compassion, and approachability, made her a beloved figure among the Icelandic public.

Even after leaving office, Finnbogadóttir remained committed to promoting education, cultural understanding, and women's rights. She continued to advocate for gender equality and served as a respected ambassador for Iceland on the global stage.

Vigdís Finnbogadóttir's legacy extends far beyond her presidency. She is remembered as a groundbreaking leader, a champion for cultural preservation, and a tireless advocate for women's empowerment. Her transformative presidency and enduring commitment to promoting Icelandic culture and gender equality have left an indelible mark on Icelandic society and continue inspiring leaders worldwide.

Part Four

Resilience in Adversity

4.1 HIDDEN FIGURES: WOMEN IN THE SHADOWS OF WAR

Codebreakers of Bletchley Park: Breaking Enigma's Secrets

The invaluable work of the women codebreakers at Bletchley Park during World War II remains an essential chapter in the history of cryptography and wartime intelligence. These remarkable women played a crucial role in deciphering encrypted messages and gathering intelligence that profoundly impacted the war's outcome.

Bletchley Park, located in England, was the leading site for British codebreakers during World War II. The facility housed brilliant minds, including mathematicians, linguists, and engineers, who were tasked with breaking the complex codes used by Axis powers, notably the German Enigma machine.

The women codebreakers at Bletchley Park made significant contributions to this monumental task. They worked tirelessly, often under intense pressure and secrecy, to decipher intercepted messages and uncover vital information. Their expertise in languages, mathematics, and pattern recognition proved instrumental in cracking the seemingly impenetrable codes.

Among the notable women at Bletchley Park were Joan Clarke, Mavis Batey, Margaret Rock, and many others. A talented mathematician, Joan Clarke played a crucial role in decrypting messages from the German Enigma machine. Mavis Batey contributed significantly to breaking the Italian naval Enigma codes, enabling Allied forces to gain a critical advantage in the Mediterranean.

The impact of the women codebreakers at Bletchley Park on the war's outcome cannot be overstated. Their deciphered messages provided valuable intelligence to the Allied forces, enabling them to anticipate enemy movements, intercept supply convoys, and gain critical insights into enemy strategies. The intelligence gathered by the codebreakers profoundly influenced numerous military operations, including the D-Day invasion and the Battle of the Atlantic.

Despite their immense contributions, the work of the women codebreakers at Bletchley Park remained largely unrecognized for several decades. Their achievements were overshadowed and often overshadowed by the male codebreakers, and their role was downplayed or omitted from historical accounts. The official secrecy surrounding Bletchley Park and the sensitive nature of the work performed there contributed to their erasure from public recognition.

However, in recent years, there has been a growing effort to highlight the contributions of these remarkable women. Their stories have been brought to light through books, documentaries, and exhibitions, shedding long-overdue recognition of their crucial role in the war effort. Their accomplishments testify to their intellect, dedication, and perseverance in the face of immense challenges.

The women codebreakers at Bletchley Park played a pivotal role in the war and paved the way for future generations of women in fields traditionally dominated by men. Their groundbreaking achievements shattered gender norms and demonstrated that women could excel in complex intellectual tasks and contribute significantly to national security matters.

Rosie the Riveters: Women in Manufacturing and Industry

During World War II, the crucial role of women workers in manufacturing and industry became evident as they stepped up to fill the gaps left by men who had joined the armed forces. The iconic figure of Rosie the Riveter came to symbolize these women who took on jobs traditionally held by men, becoming a powerful symbol of female empowerment and the changing dynamics of the workforce.

Women contributed significantly to the war effort in various industries, including aircraft manufacturing, shipbuilding, munitions production, and other vital sectors. They became riveters and welders, as well as machine operators and electricians, and worked in a wide range of skilled and semi-skilled positions. Their labor was essential for producing war materials and equipment that sustained the military and contributed to the eventual Allied victory.

One of the notable aspects of women's involvement in the war effort was their perseverance in traditionally male-dominated fields. Many of these women had limited prior experience in industrial work, but they quickly adapted to their new roles and proved their capabilities. They displayed remarkable resilience, often working long hours under challenging conditions to meet the demands of wartime production.

The contributions of women workers during World War II had a lasting impact on gender norms and workplace equality. Through their efforts, women demonstrated their competence and effectiveness in jobs traditionally considered "men's work." Their success challenged prevailing stereotypes and shattered long-held beliefs about women's abilities and limitations in the workforce.

Rosie the Riveter, with her iconic "We Can Do It!" slogan and powerful image, became a symbol of women's strength, determination, and capability. She represented the spirit of female empowerment and resilience in adversity. The idea of Rosie the Riveter has endured as a reminder of women's significant contributions during the war and their role in shaping gender norms and workplace equality.

The experiences of women workers during World War II laid the foundation for progress in women's rights and gender equality in subsequent decades. The war catalyzed change, prompting societal recognition of women's abilities and the need for expanded workforce participation. After the war, many women who had gained valuable skills and experience in industrial jobs continued to seek new opportunities and pursue careers in various fields.

The wartime experiences of women workers also influenced policies and attitudes toward gender equality in the workplace. The increased recognition of women's capabilities and contributions during the war helped pave the way for women's advancement in employment opportunities, equal pay, and workplace rights in the post-war era.

The legacy of women workers in World War II serves as a reminder of women's resilience, strength, and determination in the face of challenges and adversity. Their contributions supported the war effort and paved the way for progress in gender equality, inspiring future generations of women to pursue their aspirations and break barriers in various fields.

Night Witches: Fearless Women Pilots of the Soviet Union

During World War II, the fearless women pilots of the Soviet Union's 588th Night Bomber Regiment, famously known as the Night Witches, significantly impacted the Eastern Front. These brave women defied gender norms and played a vital role in the Soviet war effort.

The Night Witches were an all-female regiment of pilots who flew nighttime bombing missions against German targets. They earned their nickname due to the stealthy and effective tactics they employed. Flying outdated and noisy Polikarpov Po-2 biplanes made of plywood and fabric, these brave pilots conducted their operations under cover of darkness, relying on their skill, determination, and the element of surprise.

The Night Witches faced numerous challenges and dangers during their missions. Flying at low altitudes and slow speeds, they were vulnerable to enemy fire. The German soldiers nicknamed them the "Night Witches" due to the eerie sound produced by their planes, resembling the sound of a witch's broomstick. Despite these difficulties, the Night Witches persevered, demonstrating exceptional courage and skill.

The Night Witches conducted their bombing runs with remarkable precision and accuracy, targeting German positions, supply lines, and infrastructure. Their raids inflicted significant damage on the enemy while disrupting their operations. Despite the limitations of their aircraft, the Night Witches utilized their agility and knowledge of the terrain to carry out successful attacks and escape enemy retaliation.

The Night Witches' impact on the Eastern Front was substantial. Their relentless nighttime bombings disrupted German operations, causing fear and confusion among the enemy ranks. The German soldiers knew that the Night Witches were a formidable adversary and despised these courageous women's relentless and effective raids.

The Night Witches' accomplishments were not limited to their military successes. They also shattered gender stereotypes and challenged societal norms regarding women's roles during wartime. By stepping into combat roles typically reserved for men, they demonstrated that women could serve in combat positions and excel in high-pressure situations.

The Night Witches' contributions to the war effort were recognized and celebrated in the Soviet Union. They received numerous awards and honors for their bravery, skill, and dedication. The Night Witches symbolized women's empowerment and resilience, inspiring generations of women to pursue their ambitions and defy societal expectations.

Women Airforce Service Pilots (WASP): Wings for the United States

During World War II, the Women Airforce Service Pilots (WASP) played a pioneering and crucial role in the United States. These brave women, who were civilian pilots, made significant contributions to the war effort through their flying skills, aircraft ferrying, and other vital tasks.

The WASP program was established in 1942 to relieve male pilots from non-combat flying duties, freeing them up for combat missions. Over 1,000 women were accepted into the program, undergoing rigorous training to become skilled pilots. These women came from diverse backgrounds and shared a passion for aviation and a desire to contribute to the war effort.

The WASP were assigned a wide range of missions and responsibilities. They were trained to fly various types of military aircraft, including fighters, bombers, and transport planes. They were responsible for ferrying planes from factories to military bases, participating in target towing for anti-aircraft gunnery practice, testing newly overhauled aircraft, and performing other non-combat flying duties.

The skill and dedication of the WASP were invaluable. They logged thousands of flying hours, transporting aircraft across the country and playing a vital role in maintaining the flow of aircraft to support the war effort. Their contributions allowed male pilots to focus on combat missions, thereby helping to tip the scales in favor of the Allied forces.

Despite their essential role, the WASP faced numerous challenges and obstacles. They were not recognized as military members and were classified as civilian United States Army Air Forces employees. This classification meant they did not receive the same benefits and protections as their male counterparts.

The WASP also faced discrimination and prejudice within the military establishment. They had to prove themselves repeatedly, demonstrating their skills and professionalism despite skepticism and resistance from some male officers. Nevertheless, the WASP persevered, earning the respect and admiration of many for their competence and contributions.

Tragically, 38 WASP pilots lost their lives during the program's operation. Despite their sacrifice, the WASP program was disbanded in December 1944, and the women were sent home without recognition as veterans. It was not until 1977 that they were finally granted retroactive military status, and in 2009, they were awarded the Congressional Gold Medal, the highest civilian honor in the United States.

The pioneering efforts of the WASP paved the way for future generations of women in aviation. Their determination and skill helped to break down gender barriers in a traditionally male-dominated field. Their fight for recognition and veterans' rights was a significant step forward in achieving recognition for their contributions to the war effort.

The Radio Operators and Resistance Fighters: Silent Heroes of Espionage

Throughout various wars and conflicts, countless unsung heroines served as radio operators and resistance fighters, playing a vital role in transmitting information, supporting resistance movements, and displaying immense courage in the face of danger. These women, often working behind the scenes, made significant contributions to the success of resistance efforts and played a crucial role in gathering and disseminating intelligence.

During World War II, for example, women served as radio operators in resistance networks across occupied Europe. They maintained communications between resistance groups, transmitted coded messages, and coordinated actions against occupying forces. Their work was hazardous, as the enemy sought to intercept their communications and eliminate their networks.

One notable example is Britain's Special Operations Executive (SOE), which employed numerous women as radio operators in occupied territories. These women, known as "wireless operators" or "coders," were trained in wireless telegraphy, codes, and ciphers, enabling them to send and receive encrypted messages. They often worked in isolation and under constant threat of capture, torture, and execution if their activities were discovered.

Similarly, during the Vietnam War, women played significant roles as radio operators in resistance and guerrilla groups. They operated in the dense jungles, transmitting critical information to their comrades and coordinating attacks against enemy forces. These women faced harsh conditions, constant surveillance, and the ever-present risk of capture or betrayal.

In addition to their role as radio operators, these brave women often served as couriers, carrying messages, supplies, and intelligence across enemy lines. They used their ingenuity to hide radios and other communication equipment, often disguising them as everyday objects to evade detection.

The work of these radio operators and resistance fighters was essential for several reasons. First, they provided a lifeline of communication between resistance groups, allowing them to coordinate their activities, share information, and maintain morale. They played a crucial role in relaying intelligence about enemy movements, troop deployments, and strategic targets.

Second, these women were a vital link between resistance movements and the outside world. They transmitted reports and requests for support to allied forces and intelligence agencies, providing valuable insights into the resistance efforts and the conditions on the ground.

Third, their work was instrumental in shaping public opinion and rallying support for the resistance cause. Through their transmissions, they exposed the atrocities of occupying forces, provided updates on resistance activities, and shared stories of heroism and resilience. Their broadcasts and coded messages became powerful tools in inspiring hope and resistance among the oppressed populations.

Despite their risks and challenges, these women persevered, driven by a deep sense of patriotism, a commitment to their cause, and a belief in the power of information. Their contributions often went unrecognized or were overshadowed by the actions of male soldiers and leaders. However, their bravery, resourcefulness, and sacrifices should not be forgotten.

Acknowledging and honoring these unsung heroines for their vital role in resistance movements and their invaluable contribution to the cause of freedom and justice is essential. Their courage, determination, and unwavering commitment to their beliefs serve as a reminder of the extraordinary contributions that women have made and continue to make in times of conflict and struggle.

4.2 OVERCOMING ODDS: INSPIRING STORIES OF TRIUMPH

Malala Yousafzai: Voice for Girls' Education and Nobel Laureate

Malala Yousafzai's extraordinary journey is a testament to her unwavering commitment to girls' education, activism, and determination through adversity. Born on July 12, 1997, in Mingora, Pakistan, Malala grew up in the Swat Valley, where the Taliban had gained control and imposed restrictions on girls' education.

From a young age, Malala recognized the importance of education and passionately advocated for girls' rights to attend school. At just 11 years old, she began blogging anonymously for BBC Urdu under the pseudonym Gul Makai, sharing her experiences and the challenges girls face under Taliban rule. Her powerful words and fearless activism caught the international community's attention, spotlighting Pakistan's struggle for girls' education.

Tragically, in October 2012, Malala was targeted by the Taliban for her advocacy. On her way home from school, she was shot in the head and neck. Her survival was nothing short of miraculous, and her resilience only grew stronger. The assassination attempt on Malala sparked global outrage and brought attention to the urgent need for education reform and gender equality.

Following her recovery, Malala's advocacy and determination inspired people worldwide. Recognizing her unwavering commitment, she became the youngest recipient of the Nobel Peace Prize in 2014 at 17. The award recognized her bravery and brought international attention to girls' education and the importance of empowering young women.

Malala's activism extends beyond her own experiences in Pakistan. She co-founded the Malala Fund, a non-profit organization that advocates for girls' education globally. Through the fund, Malala has worked tirelessly to support education initiatives, particularly in developing countries where girls face significant barriers to accessing education.

Malala's message has resonated with millions worldwide, and she has become a prominent and influential voice for youth empowerment and social change. Her speeches, interviews, and writings consistently emphasize the transformative power of education, the need for gender equality, and the importance of standing up against injustice.

Malala's impact extends far beyond her achievements. She has inspired countless individuals, especially young girls, to pursue their dreams, fight for their rights, and overcome adversity. Her story serves as a potent reminder that even in the face of immense challenges, the voices of determined individuals can create lasting change.

Today, Malala continues to advocate for education and equality through her speaking engagements, books, and ongoing work with the Malala Fund. She has become a global icon for her courage, resilience, and unwavering commitment to ensuring that every girl has access to quality education and the opportunity to fulfill her potential.

Malala Yousafzai's extraordinary journey reminds us of the power of education, the importance of fighting for gender equality, and the need to empower young people to become catalysts for change. Her story inspires individuals and communities worldwide, urging us to join her in the fight for a more equitable and just world.

Helen Keller: Overcoming Deaf-Blindness to Inspire the World

Helen Keller's remarkable life is a testament to the indomitable human spirit and the power of perseverance. Born on June 27, 1880, in Tuscumbia, Alabama, Keller lost both her vision and hearing at 19 months due to an illness believed to be scarlet fever or meningitis. Despite these profound disabilities, Keller overcame immense challenges to become a trailblazing advocate, writer, and speaker.

Keller's life changed at 6 when Anne Sullivan became her teacher and mentor. Through Sullivan's tireless efforts, Keller learned to communicate using a manual alphabet, tactile sign language, and later Braille. Sullivan's guidance and Keller's determination opened up a new world, allowing her to develop language skills and access knowledge and ideas.

Keller's thirst for knowledge led her to pursue education and attend Radcliffe College. She became the first deafblind person to earn a Bachelor of Arts degree. She forged a remarkable career as a writer, speaker, and advocate for the rights of people with disabilities.

Keller's writings, including her autobiography "The Story of My Life," touched readers' hearts worldwide. Her eloquence and profound insights into the human condition captivated audiences and demonstrated the power of words and ideas. Through her writing, Keller shared her experiences, struggles, and triumphs, shedding light on the challenges faced by people with disabilities and promoting understanding and empathy.

Keller's advocacy work extended beyond her writing. She became a vocal champion for disability rights, fighting for improved access to education, employment opportunities, and social inclusion for individuals with disabilities. Keller's influence helped change societal perceptions of disability and paved the way for advancements in disability rights and inclusive education.

Throughout her life, Keller tirelessly traveled the world, delivering speeches and lectures that inspired audiences and challenged societal prejudices. Her powerful message emphasized the importance of determination, self-advocacy, and the inherent worth of every individual, regardless of their disabilities.

Keller's impact on society was far-reaching. She played a pivotal role in changing perceptions about people with disabilities, proving they can lead fulfilling lives, contribute to society, and overcome seemingly insurmountable obstacles. Her legacy continues to inspire generations of individuals with disabilities, as well as those without disabilities, to embrace empathy, compassion, and the pursuit of knowledge.

In recognition of her extraordinary achievements, Keller received numerous awards and honors throughout her life, including the Presidential Medal of Freedom, one of the highest civilian awards in the United States. She remains an enduring symbol of resilience, perseverance, and the unlimited potential of the human spirit.

Helen Keller's life inspires millions, reminding us of the power of determination, the importance of education, and the need for inclusivity and equal rights for all individuals. Her legacy continues to shape our understanding of disability, ignite social change, and remind us that remarkable achievements are possible with determination, compassion, and unwavering belief in oneself.

Harriet Tubman: Abolitionist, Freedom Fighter, and Underground Railroad Conductor

Harriet Tubman's life is a testament to bravery, resilience, and unwavering commitment to justice. Born into slavery around 1822 in Maryland, Tubman endured the hardships and cruelty of bondage before escaping to freedom herself. However, she did not stop there. Tubman became one of the most renowned conductors of the Underground Railroad, leading countless enslaved individuals to liberty and actively participating in the abolitionist movement.

Tubman's journey to freedom began in 1849 when she dared to escape slavery. With great determination, she embarked on a treacherous 100-mile journey, navigating hostile territories and evading capture. This escape marked the beginning of her life as a freedom fighter.

After reaching safety, Tubman became increasingly aware of the plight of those left behind in bondage. Driven by a deep sense of justice and empathy, she dedicated herself to helping others escape the chains of slavery. Tubman became a fearless conductor of the Underground Railroad, a network of secret routes and safe houses that facilitated the escape of enslaved individuals to free states and Canada. Despite the constant threat to her life, Tubman made multiple dangerous journeys back into slave-holding states, leading approximately 70 enslaved individuals, including family members and strangers, to freedom.

Tubman's methods were as ingenious as they were courageous. She used her knowledge of the landscape, ability to read the stars, and intimate familiarity with the Underground Railroad network to navigate the perilous paths to freedom. Tubman's unwavering determination, resourcefulness, and remarkable ability to elude capture earned her the nickname "Moses," as she led her people out of bondage, just as the biblical figure had led the Israelites to freedom.

Beyond her role as a conductor, Tubman was actively involved in the abolitionist movement and worked alongside prominent figures such as Frederick Douglass. She participated in various activities, including speaking engagements, fundraisers, and organizing efforts to support the cause. Tubman's bravery, resilience, and powerful presence left an indelible impact on those who crossed her path and inspired countless others to join the fight against slavery and inequality.

Tubman's contributions extended beyond the Underground Railroad and the abolitionist movement. During the Civil War, she served as a nurse, cook, and spy for the Union Army, demonstrating her unwavering commitment to the cause of freedom and justice. Tubman's services provided vital intelligence to Union forces, contributing to strategic victories and saving lives.

Throughout her life, Tubman never wavered in her pursuit of justice. She firmly believed in the equality and dignity of every individual and actively fought against racism, discrimination, and inequality. Even after slavery was officially abolished with the Emancipation Proclamation and the ratification of the Thirteenth Amendment, Tubman continued to advocate for the rights of African Americans, women's suffrage, and social justice.

Harriet Tubman's legacy is one of courage, determination, and unyielding resistance. Her extraordinary personal liberation story and tireless efforts to liberate others from the bonds of slavery have inspired generations. Tubman's name has become synonymous with freedom, and her memory serves as a reminder of the power of one person's unwavering dedication to justice and the transformative impact that can be achieved.

Harriet Tubman is celebrated as an American hero for her remarkable achievements. Her contributions to the fight against slavery, her leadership in the Underground Railroad, and her lifelong commitment to equality and justice make her an enduring symbol of hope and resilience.

Junko Tabei: Conquering Everest and Breaking Gender Barriers

Junko Tabei's achievements as a mountaineer are a testament to her courage, determination, and trailblazing spirit. Born in Japan in 1939, Tabei developed a passion for climbing at a young age. Despite societal expectations and limited opportunities for women in the male-dominated field of mountaineering, she pursued her dreams relentlessly.

Tabei's most notable accomplishment came in 1975 when she became the first woman to reach Mount Everest's summit, the world's highest peak. Her successful ascent was a groundbreaking achievement that shattered gender barriers and paved the way for future generations of female climbers.

Tabei's journey to Everest was not without challenges. She faced numerous obstacles, including limited financial resources, societal prejudice, and the logistical difficulties of organizing an expedition. However, her unwavering determination propelled her forward. Tabei formed the Ladies' Climbing Club in 1969, which supported and encouraged women interested in mountaineering. Through this club, she gained the necessary experience and built a network of fellow climbers who shared her passion.

On May 16, 1975, Tabei and her team embarked on their Everest expedition. She pushed forward despite adverse weather conditions and treacherous terrain, demonstrating remarkable physical and mental strength. After weeks of strenuous climbing, Tabei reached the summit of Mount Everest, etching her name in history as the first woman to accomplish this feat. Her success inspired countless women worldwide to pursue their dreams and challenge societal expectations.

Tabei's achievements extended far beyond Mount Everest. She continued to climb numerous peaks worldwide, including the Seven Summits, the highest mountain on each continent. She also became the first woman to reach the summit of the highest peaks in over 70 countries. Tabei's mountaineering accomplishments were a testament to her skill, resilience, and passion for exploration.

In addition to her achievements, Tabei advocated for equal opportunities for women in climbing, encouraging them to push their limits and pursue their aspirations. Tabei believed mountaineering offered valuable lessons in self-discovery, resilience, and teamwork, essential for personal growth and empowerment.

Tabei's legacy as a pioneering female mountaineer continues to inspire generations of women. Her courage and determination demonstrated that gender should not be a barrier to pursuing one's passions and achieving extraordinary goals. Tabei challenged societal norms through her achievements and showed the world that women could excel in traditionally male-dominated fields.

Even after her passing in 2016, Tabei's legacy lives on. Her contributions to mountaineering and her advocacy for gender equality have left an indelible mark on the climbing community. She has inspired countless women to break barriers, set their records, and conquer their metaphorical mountains.

Junko Tabei's remarkable journey from humble beginnings to becoming the first woman to summit Mount Everest is a powerful reminder of the human spirit's ability to overcome obstacles. Her achievements inspire individuals of all backgrounds to challenge limitations, pursue their passions, and leave their mark on the world.

Maya Angelou: Poet, Author, and Voice of Resilience

Maya Angelou was a renowned poet, author, and civil rights activist whose life and work impacted literature and the pursuit of equality and empowerment. Born Marguerite Annie Johnson on April 4, 1928, in St. Louis, Missouri, Angelou overcame a tumultuous childhood to become one of the most celebrated voices of her generation.

Angelou's literary contributions are marked by her eloquence, depth of emotion, and poignant storytelling. Her best-known work, "I Know Why the Caged Bird Sings," published in 1969, is a memoir that chronicles her experiences growing up in the racially segregated South. The book's frank exploration of racism, trauma, and identity resonated deeply with readers and established Angelou as a powerful and influential writer. Her poetic style, infused with vivid imagery and rhythm, captivated audiences and brought to life the struggles and triumphs of the African American experience.

Throughout her career, Angelou authored numerous books, including poetry collections like "And Still I Rise," "Phenomenal Woman," and "The Complete Collected Poems of Maya Angelou." Her prose works, such as "Gather Together in My Name" and "A Song Flung Up to Heaven," further showcased her storytelling prowess and ability to delve into complex themes with grace and insight. Angelou's writing addressed race, gender, love, and personal growth, inviting readers to reflect on their experiences and find strength in adversity.

Angelou's resilience in overcoming personal struggles was a defining characteristic of her life and work. She endured a traumatic childhood, including the impact of racial discrimination, and at the age of eight, she was sexually assaulted by her mother's boyfriend. This traumatic event led to her becoming mute for several years, during which time she found solace in literature and the power of words. Through her writing and public speaking, Angelou channeled her experiences into a message of resilience, self-acceptance, and hope, inspiring countless individuals to rise above their challenges.

In addition to her literary accomplishments, Angelou was a prominent civil rights activist. She worked alongside prominent figures such as Dr. Martin Luther King Jr. and Malcolm X, lending her voice to the struggle for racial equality and social justice. Her involvement in the civil rights movement and her work as a journalist and actress demonstrated her commitment to using her platform to effect meaningful change.

Angelou's impact extended beyond her writing and activism. Her powerful stage presence and captivating performances as a poet and public speaker garnered widespread acclaim. She delivered a memorable reading of her poem "On the Pulse of Morning" at President Bill Clinton's inauguration in 1993, becoming the first poet since Robert Frost to participate in such a significant event. Her oratory skills and ability to connect with audiences on a deep emotional level made her a revered and influential figure.

Maya Angelou's contributions to literature, civil rights, and promoting equality and empowerment have made her iconic. Her words inspire and resonate with readers of all backgrounds, offering insights into the human experience and encouraging empathy, understanding, and compassion. Her life and work remind us of the power of storytelling, the strength of the human spirit, and the importance of using our voices to effect positive change in the world. Maya Angelou's legacy is a testament to the transformative power of literature and the enduring impact of a resilient and compassionate soul.

4.3 TRAILBLAZERS IN SPORTS AND ATHLETICS

Wilma Rudolph: Triumph over Adversity in Track and Field

Wilma Rudolph's journey from a childhood plagued by adversity and physical challenges to becoming an Olympic champion is truly inspiring. Born June 23, 1940, in Saint Bethlehem, Tennessee, Rudolph faced numerous obstacles in her early years. She was born prematurely and contracted polio at the age of four, which resulted in paralysis of her left leg. Rudolph's indomitable spirit and unwavering determination propelled her toward greatness despite these setbacks.

Rudolph's love for sports and her desire to overcome her physical limitations became evident as she underwent rigorous treatments and therapy for her leg. With the support of her family, she took her first steps without assistance at the age of eight, defying the odds and embarking on a path that would lead her to athletic glory.

Rudolph's incredible talent in track and field soon became apparent. She joined her high school track team, quickly becoming a standout athlete. Her remarkable speed and agility caught the attention of coaches and scouts, and she soon began competing nationally.

At 16, Rudolph made her mark on the international stage when she competed in the 1956 Melbourne Olympics. Although she did not win a medal, her performances garnered attention and set the stage for her future successes.

Four years later, at the 1960 Rome Olympics, Rudolph's extraordinary abilities propelled her to greatness. She became the first American woman to win three gold medals in track and field at a single Olympic Games. Rudolph's victories came in the 100-meter, 200-meter, and 4x100-meter relay events, where she showcased her lightning-fast speed and flawless technique. Her accomplishments were even more impressive because she set a new world record in the 200-meter race.

Rudolph's achievements in Rome cemented her status as an Olympic legend and inspired millions worldwide. She symbolized resilience and determination, proving that perseverance and hard work can overcome even the most challenging circumstances.

Beyond her Olympic triumphs, Rudolph continued to excel in her athletic career. She went on to break multiple records and received numerous accolades. Her impact extended beyond the track as she became an influential figure, advocating for racial and gender equality in sports.

Rudolph's success paved the way for future generations of African American athletes and inspired young girls worldwide to pursue their dreams. Her achievements demonstrated that one's background and physical limitations need not hinder success.

In recognition of her remarkable athletic career and significant contributions to society, Rudolph was inducted into the National Track and Field Hall of Fame and the U.S. Olympic Hall of Fame. She later dedicated her life to community service, promoting education and opportunities for underprivileged youth.

Althea Gibson: The First African American Grand Slam Champion

Althea Gibson's accomplishments in tennis broke barriers and paved the way for racial integration in the sport. Born on August 25, 1927, in Silver, South Carolina, Gibson's journey to becoming a tennis legend was marked by talent, determination, and a relentless pursuit of excellence.

In the era of segregation and racial discrimination, Gibson faced numerous challenges in pursuing her passion for tennis. However, her immense athletic talent and relentless drive propelled her to overcome these obstacles and make history on the tennis court.

Gibson's breakthrough came in 1950 when she became the first African American player to compete in the United States Lawn Tennis Association (USLTA) national championship. This marked a significant milestone in the sport as she challenged the racially segregated tennis world.

In the subsequent years, Gibson's dominance in tennis became evident as she achieved remarkable success. In 1956, she made history by becoming the first African American woman to win a Grand Slam title when she triumphed at the French Championships (now known as the French Open) in both singles and doubles events. She followed this groundbreaking victory with another triumph at the Wimbledon Championships in 1957, becoming the first African American woman to win the prestigious tournament.

Gibson's athletic prowess and exceptional skill on the tennis court captivated audiences around the world. Her powerful serve, lightning-fast reflexes, and aggressive playing style made her a formidable competitor. She displayed incredible versatility, excelling in both singles and doubles matches.

Beyond her accomplishments, Gibson also significantly contributed to the sport as a trailblazer for racial integration. Her success challenged the prevailing racial barriers in tennis and inspired other African American athletes to pursue their dreams. Through her perseverance and achievements, Gibson helped break down the walls of segregation in tennis, opening doors for future generations of players of color.

Gibson's impact extended beyond the tennis court. Her groundbreaking achievements were recognized and celebrated worldwide, and she became a symbol of empowerment and inspiration for African Americans and aspiring athletes everywhere. Her success challenged racial prejudice and helped reshape the perception of African American athletes in mainstream sports.

Although Gibson retired from professional tennis in 1958, her legacy as a trailblazer and pioneer in the sport endured. She left an indelible mark on tennis history and inspired generations of players who followed in her footsteps.

In recognition of her contributions to the sport, Gibson was inducted into the International Tennis Hall of Fame in 1971. Her remarkable achievements continue to be celebrated, and her legacy serves as a reminder of the power of perseverance, courage, and determination in the face of adversity.

Althea Gibson's journey and triumphs in tennis transformed the sport, broke racial barriers, and inspired generations of athletes. Her pioneering spirit and unwavering commitment to excellence will be remembered as she remains an icon of courage, talent, and resilience in tennis.

Babe Didrikson Zaharias: Multisport Champion and Barrier Breaker

Babe Didrikson Zaharias, born on June 26, 1911, in Port Arthur, Texas, was a trailblazing athlete who achieved remarkable success in multiple sports, defying societal expectations and breaking barriers. Her versatility, unmatched talent, and unwavering determination established her as one of the greatest athletes of the 20th century.

Zaharias's athletic prowess first gained recognition in track and field. She competed in the 1932 Olympics in Los Angeles, winning two gold medals and one silver medal in the javelin throw, hurdles, and high jump, respectively. Her extraordinary performances showcased her exceptional speed, agility, and strength.

In addition to track and field, Zaharias made her mark in basketball, becoming a standout player in the Amateur Athletic Union (AAU). She led her team, the Employers Casualty Company, to multiple national championships and earned widespread acclaim for her scoring ability and dominant presence on the court.

However, it was in golf that Zaharias left her indelible mark. Despite being relatively new to the sport, she quickly rose to prominence and redefined women's golf. Zaharias's aggressive playing style, powerful drives, and exceptional putting skills revolutionized the game.

In 1945, she won the Women's National Open, a precursor to the modern-day U.S. Women's Open, by a staggering 12 strokes. This victory marked the beginning of her illustrious golf career. Zaharias won 10 major championships, including three U.S. Women's Open titles, and became the first American woman to win the British Ladies Amateur.

Zaharias's athletic achievements were not limited to her extraordinary skills; she also shattered societal barriers. In a time when women's sports received limited attention and resources, Zaharias became a beacon of inspiration for female athletes. She defied stereotypes, challenging traditional gender roles and proving that women could compete at the highest level in sports.

Zaharias's impact extended beyond her athletic prowess. Her charismatic personality, engaging with both fans and the media, helped popularize women's sports and brought attention to the achievements of female athletes. She played a pivotal role in establishing the Ladies Professional Golf Association (LPGA) in 1950, which provided opportunities for women to compete professionally and paved the way for future generations of female golfers.

Tragically, Zaharias's career was interrupted by a battle with cancer. Despite undergoing multiple surgeries, she triumphantly returned to golf and continued to compete at a high level. Her resilience and determination in the face of adversity inspired countless individuals worldwide.

Babe Didrikson Zaharias's enduring impact on women's sports cannot be overstated. Her exceptional athletic ability, groundbreaking achievements, and unwavering determination opened doors for women in sports and challenged societal norms. Zaharias's legacy inspires generations of female athletes, reminding them they can excel in any sport and break through barriers.

In recognition of her contributions to sports, Zaharias was posthumously awarded the Presidential Medal of Freedom, the highest civilian honor in the United States. She was also inducted into multiple Halls of Fame, including the World Golf Hall of Fame and the Women's Sports Hall of Fame.

Gertrude Ederle: The First Woman to Swim the English Channel

Gertrude Ederle, born on October 23, 1905, in New York City, made history as a pioneering swimmer and athlete, breaking barriers and setting records in the swimming world. Her groundbreaking feat of becoming the first woman to swim the English Channel solidified her legacy as one of the most influential figures in women's sports.

Ederle's swimming career began at a young age when she joined the Women's Swimming Association (WSA) in New York. Under the guidance of her coach, Charlotte Epstein, Ederle quickly demonstrated her exceptional talent and determination in the pool. Her hard work and dedication paid off when, at 16, she competed in the 1924 Olympics in Paris, winning a gold medal as part of the 4x100-meter freestyle relay team and two bronze medals in individual events.

However, Ederle's historic swim across the English Channel on August 6, 1926, brought her worldwide acclaim. The English Channel, a treacherous body of water separating England and France, had been conquered by only a handful of men at the time. Ederle set out to defy the odds and make her mark in history.

Facing strong currents, cold water, and relentless challenges, Ederle swam for 14 hours and 34 minutes, crossing the English Channel and shattering the existing record by more than two hours. Her remarkable achievement not only made headlines worldwide but also inspired a generation of female athletes and challenged prevailing notions of women's capabilities in sports.

Ederle's historic swim was a turning point in women's sports, signaling a shift toward greater recognition and acceptance of women's athletic abilities. Her success sparked widespread interest in swimming and motivated many young women to pursue their goals in the sport. Ederle became an icon, representing the limitless potential of female athletes and the breaking down gender barriers.

Following her English Channel triumph, Ederle continued to set records and inspire others in the swimming world. She set numerous world records in various distances and stroke styles, further solidifying her status as one of the greatest swimmers of her time. Ederle's influence extended beyond her achievements, as she paved the way for increased participation and recognition of women in swimming and other sports.

Ederle's accomplishments showcased her extraordinary talent and highlighted her determination and resilience. Throughout her career, she faced various challenges, including hearing impairment resulting from childhood measles, but she never let these obstacles hinder her pursuit of greatness. Ederle's indomitable spirit and refusal to be limited by societal expectations made her a role model for generations of female athletes.

Beyond her achievements in the pool, Ederle's impact on women's sports reverberated through her later endeavors. She dedicated herself to teaching swimming and promoting water safety among children. Her passion for swimming and commitment to helping others learn and enjoy the sport contributed to the growth and accessibility of swimming for women and men alike.

Alice Coachman: Trailblazer in Olympic Track and Field

Alice Coachman, born on November 9, 1923, in Albany, Georgia, made history as a trailblazing athlete and the first African American woman to win an Olympic gold medal in track and field. Her exceptional accomplishments in the high jump event, perseverance in the face of discrimination, and enduring legacy as an inspiration to future generations have cemented her place in sports history.

Coachman's athletic journey began in childhood, where she developed a passion for running and jumping. She honed her skills in track and field while attending the Tuskegee Institute in Alabama, where she trained under her coach, Walter Davis.

In 1948, Coachman made her mark on the international stage when she competed in the Olympic Games in London. Despite racial prejudice and limited opportunities for training and competition due to segregation in the United States, Coachman's talent and determination propelled her to unprecedented heights.

In the high jump event, Coachman soared to new heights, clearing a height of 1.68 meters (5 feet 6 1/8 inches) to secure the gold medal. Her remarkable performance made her the first African American woman to win an Olympic gold medal and set a new Olympic record.

Coachman's Olympic triumph was a significant milestone for African American athletes and women in sports. Her victory challenged the stereotypes and barriers marginalized people of color and women faced in athletics. Coachman's accomplishments empowered countless individuals, proving that talent and perseverance could overcome systemic prejudice and discrimination.

Beyond her Olympic success, Coachman continued to excel in her athletic career. She set multiple records in the high jump and won 10 consecutive national championships from 1939 to 1948. Her dominance in the sport solidified her status as one of the best high jumpers of her time.

Coachman's impact extended beyond the track and field arena. Her achievements helped pave the way for future generations of African American athletes, opening doors and challenging societal norms regarding race and gender in sports. Her success was a beacon of hope and inspiration for aspiring athletes, demonstrating that talent and determination could break down barriers and shatter stereotypes.

Despite facing numerous challenges, including limited access to training facilities and racial discrimination, Coachman never wavered in her pursuit of excellence. Her resilience, tenacity, and unwavering commitment to her sport have made her an enduring role model for athletes worldwide.

After retiring from competitive athletics, Coachman dedicated herself to education and community service. She founded the Alice Coachman Track and Field Foundation to provide young athletes, particularly girls, opportunities to pursue their athletic dreams.

Alice Coachman's groundbreaking accomplishments as the first African American woman to win an Olympic gold medal in track and field, her record-breaking high jump performances, and her unwavering determination in the face of adversity continue to inspire and empower individuals today. Her legacy is a reminder that the pursuit of excellence knows no boundaries and that true greatness is achieved through talent, perseverance, and the courage to challenge societal norms.

Part Five

Voices from the Margins

5.1 WOMEN OF COLOR: RECLAIMING THEIR NARRATIVES

Sojourner Truth: Activist and Abolitionist

Sojourner Truth, born into slavery as Isabella Baumfree in 1797, emerged as a remarkable figure in fighting against slavery, women's rights, and social justice. Her life and activism continue to inspire generations with her powerful oratory skills, unwavering determination, and commitment to equality.

Truth's journey to becoming a prominent abolitionist and women's rights advocate began with her escape from slavery in 1826. After gaining her freedom, she dedicated her life to fighting against the institution of slavery and advocating for the rights of African Americans.

One of Truth's most famous speeches, "Ain't I a Woman?" was delivered at the Women's Convention in Akron, Ohio, in 1851. In this dynamic address, she eloquently challenged prevailing notions of gender and race, advocating for equal rights for women and African Americans. Her speech highlighted the intersectionality of gender and race, emphasizing the importance of recognizing the struggles faced by Black women.

Truth's powerful oratory skills and her experiences as a formerly enslaved person made her a compelling advocate for the abolitionist movement. She traveled extensively, delivering speeches that moved audiences and inspired action. Her words resonated with many and helped humanize the struggles and aspirations of enslaved individuals.

In addition to her activism against slavery, Truth fought for women's rights, particularly the right to vote. She believed that women should have equal rights and opportunities as men, and she actively participated in suffrage conventions and advocated for women's suffrage until her death.

Truth's activism and advocacy extended beyond her powerful speeches. She actively supported and aided those seeking freedom, including serving as a recruiter for the Union Army during the Civil War and working with freedmen and freedwomen after the Emancipation Proclamation.

Sojourner Truth's contributions to the abolitionist movement, her powerful "Ain't I a Woman?" speech, and her steadfast commitment to social justice impacted American history. Her words and actions challenged societal norms and paved the way for future generations in the fight against slavery, gender inequality, and racial injustice.

Her legacy continues to inspire and inform social justice movements today. Truth's courage, resilience, and determination in the face of adversity serve as a reminder that the voices of the marginalized and oppressed can create lasting change. Her advocacy for the rights of African Americans and women helped lay the foundation for a more inclusive and equitable society.

Sojourner Truth's life and activism serve as a testament to the power of speaking truth to power, the importance of intersectional activism, and the enduring impact one individual can have on the quest for freedom, justice, and equality.

Frida Kahlo: The Unyielding Spirit of Mexican Art

Frida Kahlo, born Magdalena Carmen Frida Kahlo y Calderón on July 6, 1907, in Coyoacán, Mexico, was a visionary artist whose work continues to captivate and inspire audiences worldwide. Kahlo's art is characterized by her powerful self-portraits, which explore identity, femininity, pain, and resilience.

Kahlo's unique artistic style is often associated with surrealism, although she preferred to describe her art as "realist." Drawing inspiration from Mexican folk art and culture, she incorporated vibrant colors, intricate details, and symbolism into her paintings. Kahlo's works often feature flowers, animals, and traditional Mexican clothing, reflecting her deep connection to Mexican heritage and folklore.

One of the defining aspects of Kahlo's art is her use of self-portraiture. Through her self-portraits, Kahlo expressed her innermost emotions, struggles, and experiences. She unflinchingly depicted her physical and emotional pain resulting from a bus accident in her youth, which left her with lifelong health issues. Kahlo's self-portraits became a means of reclaiming her narrative and asserting her identity in a world that often marginalized women and people of color.

Beyond her artistic prowess, Frida Kahlo's cultural influence was pivotal in challenging traditional gender norms and asserting female autonomy and agency. Kahlo subverted conventional portrayals of women in art through her depictions of the female form and her exploration of feminine experiences. Her unapologetic representation of her body and experiences inspired countless women, encouraging them to embrace their uniqueness and challenge societal expectations.

Kahlo's art explored cultural identity and pride themes as a woman of mixed heritage. She celebrated her Mexican roots and used her work as a platform to challenge cultural assimilation and promote a sense of cultural belonging. Kahlo's artistic expression became a powerful tool for reclaiming and celebrating marginalized identities.

Frida Kahlo's significance as a symbol of empowerment for women and people of color extends far beyond the art world. Her resilience in the face of physical and emotional challenges, her fierce determination to assert her individuality, and her unapologetic portrayal of her experiences continue to resonate with audiences. Kahlo's art serves as a reminder of the power of self-expression, the importance of embracing one's identity, and the potential for art to ignite social change.

In contemporary culture, Frida Kahlo remains an enduring icon. Her image adorns countless posters, fashion items, and artworks, solidifying her status as a global symbol of strength, authenticity, and empowerment. Her legacy continues to inspire artists, feminists, and individuals from diverse backgrounds, offering a powerful reminder of the transformative power of art and the enduring impact of an artist who fearlessly shared her truth with the world.

Shirley Chisholm: Pioneering Politician and Advocate for Equality

Shirley Anita Chisholm, born November 30, 1924, in Brooklyn, New York, was a pioneering figure in American politics. Her groundbreaking career and tireless advocacy made her a prominent leader in the fight for civil rights, gender equality, and social justice.

Chisholm's political journey began when she was elected to the New York State Assembly in 1964, becoming the second African American woman to serve in the state legislature. 1968 she made history by becoming the first African American woman elected to the United States Congress, representing New York's 12th congressional district. Throughout her time in Congress, Chisholm championed numerous progressive causes, including education reform, affordable housing, and social welfare programs.

As a member of the Congressional Black Caucus, Chisholm worked tirelessly to advance civil rights and promote equality. She became a vocal advocate for gender and racial equality, using her platform to challenge discriminatory practices and call for better representation of marginalized communities in government and society. Chisholm famously stated, "If they don't give you a seat at the table, bring a folding chair," encapsulating her determination to break down barriers and empower marginalized voices.

In 1972, Chisholm made history again by becoming the first major-party African American candidate for President of the United States, running for the Democratic nomination. Her campaign focused on progressive policies, such as affordable healthcare, increased access to education, and social justice reforms. While her bid for the presidency was unsuccessful, Chisholm's campaign paved the way for future African American and female candidates, inspiring a new generation of leaders.

Chisholm's contributions to civil rights and unwavering dedication to equality have left an indelible mark on American politics. She challenged the status quo and fought against entrenched oppression, leaving a legacy of courage and resilience. Her commitment to intersectional activism, recognizing the overlapping struggles faced by women of color, helped shape the modern discourse on social justice and equality.

Throughout her career, Chisholm faced numerous obstacles and endured harsh criticism, yet she remained steadfast in her pursuit of justice. Her legacy as a pioneer and trailblazer continues to inspire generations of politicians, activists, and ordinary citizens. Chisholm's impact is felt in politics, civil rights, and the broader fight for equality and representation. She shattered glass ceilings, challenged systemic inequalities, and empowered marginalized communities, leaving an enduring imprint on the fabric of American society.

Maya Angelou: Voice of Strength and Resilience

Maya Angelou, born Marguerite Annie Johnson on April 4, 1928, in St. Louis, Missouri, was a literary icon, civil rights activist, and an influential voice for African Americans and women of color. Her life and work continue to inspire and resonate with audiences worldwide.

Angelou's literary achievements are vast and diverse. She is best known for her autobiographical work, "I Know Why the Caged Bird Sings," published in 1969. This groundbreaking memoir courageously explored themes of racism, identity, and resilience, becoming an instant classic. Angelou's lyrical prose, honest storytelling, and powerful portrayal of her personal experiences captured the hearts and minds of readers, establishing her as a prominent voice in American literature.

Beyond her memoir, Angelou's body of work encompassed poetry, essays, plays, and screenplays. Her poetry collections, such as "And Still I Rise" and "Phenomenal Woman," showcased her masterful use of language, rhythm, and imagery to address themes of love, empowerment, and social justice. Her words resonated with millions, offering solace, strength, and inspiration in the face of adversity.

Angelou's profound impact on promoting equality and empowerment extended beyond her literary achievements. She was an outspoken advocate for civil rights, lending her voice and influence to the fight against racial discrimination and social injustice. She worked closely with prominent civil rights leaders like Martin Luther King Jr. and Malcolm X, using her art and activism to amplify their messages of equality and freedom.

As a woman of color, Angelou played a crucial role in breaking down barriers and providing representation for marginalized communities. The unapologetic embrace of her identity and her exploration of black womanhood challenged societal norms and inspired countless women to embrace their power and worth. Angelou's writings celebrated the beauty and strength of blackness while shedding light on the unique struggles faced by women of color in a predominantly white society.

Angelou's influence extended beyond literature and activism. Her powerful voice and magnetic presence made her a sought-after speaker and performer. She delivered powerful speeches, including the memorable recitation of her poem "On the Pulse of Morning" at President Bill Clinton's inauguration in 1993. Her performances on stage and screen showcased her multifaceted talents and brought her messages of hope, resilience, and empowerment to even wider audiences.

Maya Angelou's impact as a writer, poet, and civil rights activist cannot be overstated. Her contributions to literature, her unyielding pursuit of equality, and her fearless advocacy for the rights of marginalized communities have left an indelible mark on society. She used her words to uplift, educate, and inspire, providing a voice for those silenced and marginalized.

Patsy Mink: Champion for Women's Rights and Education

During her remarkable career, Patsy Mink was a politician and advocate who significantly contributed to women's rights, education, and equality. As the first woman of color elected to the United States Congress, she shattered barriers and fought tirelessly for gender equality and social justice.

Born on December 6, 1927, in Maui, Hawaii, Patsy Mink faced discrimination and inequality firsthand, which fueled her passion for activism. She was inspired by her own experiences as a Japanese-American woman and her family's struggles during World War II internment. Mink's determination to challenge the status quo and create positive change guided her throughout her life.

In 1965, Mink made history by becoming the first woman of color elected to the U.S. Congress, representing Hawaii's first congressional district. During her time in Congress, she championed numerous vital causes, notably her work on education and gender equality. Mink recognized education's critical role in empowering individuals and communities and became a leading advocate for educational access and equity.

One of Mink's most significant achievements was co-authoring Title IX of the Education Amendments Act of 1972. This landmark legislation prohibited sex discrimination in education, opening doors for women and girls to participate in sports, receive equal educational opportunities, and combat gender-based discrimination on campuses across the United States. Mink's dedication to gender equality and her instrumental role in shaping Title IX had a profound and lasting impact on the lives of countless women and girls.

Throughout her career, Mink fought against gender discrimination in various forms. She advocated for policies that promoted pay equity, reproductive rights, and affordable childcare. Mink also supported and mentored numerous women seeking to enter politics, encouraging them to follow in her footsteps and create positive change within the system.

Patsy Mink's legacy as a trailblazer for women in politics and a champion of gender equality continues to resonate today. Her unwavering commitment to justice and fairness laid the groundwork for educational progress, equal opportunity, and representation. Mink's tireless efforts inspired generations of women to challenge barriers and make their voices heard in the political sphere.

Sadly, Patsy Mink passed away on September 28, 2002, but her impact and legacy live on. Her pioneering spirit, determination, and dedication to equality inspire individuals and communities to advocate for social change. Through her groundbreaking achievements and unwavering advocacy, Patsy Mink left an indelible mark on American politics and society, forever cementing her place as a champion for women's rights and a trailblazer for women of color in the United States.

5.3 AMPLIFYING INDIGENOUS VOICES

Malinche: Interpreting Cultures and Indigenous Identity

Malinche, also known as Doña Marina, occupies a complex and controversial historical place as a Nahua woman who played a significant role during the Spanish conquest of the Aztec Empire. Her story raises essential discussions about the complexities of identity, cultural exchange, and the power dynamics that unfolded during this tumultuous period.

Malinche's involvement in the Spanish conquest occurred in the early 16th century when Hernán Cortés and his expedition arrived in Mesoamerica. As a Nahua woman, she was originally from the Gulf Coast region of Mexico and was later sold into slavery. She eventually became a translator and advisor to Cortés, assisting in communication between the Spanish and indigenous peoples, including the Aztecs.

Malinche's linguistic skills and knowledge of the indigenous cultures proved invaluable to Cortés and the Spanish conquistadors. Her ability to bridge the language barrier and provide insights into the Aztec Empire's politics and alliances gave the Spanish a significant advantage. She played a crucial role in establishing diplomatic relations, negotiating alliances with indigenous groups who were enemies of the Aztecs, and interpreting during critical encounters and battles.

The historical context surrounding Malinche's involvement is complex. The Spanish conquest of the Aztec Empire brought profound changes to Mesoamerican societies, including introducing European diseases, imposition of Spanish rule, and disrupting existing power structures. Some indigenous communities viewed the arrival of the Spanish as an opportunity to resist Aztec dominance. In contrast, others saw it as a devastating intrusion on their way of life.

Malinche's role as an intermediary between the Spanish and indigenous populations has led to ongoing debates and varying interpretations of her legacy. She has been both praised and vilified throughout history. Some view her as a traitor, accusing her of betraying her people by aligning with the Spanish conquerors. Others see her as a survivor navigating a complex and dangerous situation, using her skills to secure her survival and protect her people as best she could.

It is essential to consider the power dynamics at play during this time. As a woman and an enslaved person, Malinche had limited agency and faced considerable coercion and subjugation. While she had a role in facilitating the Spanish conquest, her agency and motives are often debated. Some argue she made the best of a difficult situation, using her intelligence and survival instincts to navigate an unfamiliar and dangerous world.

Malinche's legacy is intertwined with the more extensive history of colonialism, cultural assimilation, and the erasure of indigenous cultures. Her story raises important questions about the impact of colonization on indigenous peoples and the complexities of identity and cultural exchange.

It is crucial to recognize that Malinche's story is often told through the lens of European colonization, and many indigenous perspectives have been marginalized or lost over time. As contemporary scholars and historians continue to revisit and reassess this period, efforts are made to elevate indigenous voices and perspectives. This provides a more nuanced understanding of Malinche's role and the impact of the Spanish conquest on Mesoamerican societies.

In conclusion, the role of Malinche, or Doña Marina, in the Spanish conquest of the Aztec Empire is complex. Her involvement as an interpreter and advisor to Hernán Cortés raises questions about agency, power dynamics, and cultural exchange. Her story serves as a reminder of the complexities and legacies of colonialism and the ongoing debates surrounding the historical narrative of indigenous women caught between cultures.

Winona LaDuke: Environmental Activism and Indigenous Rights

Winona LaDuke, an Anishinaabe activist, environmentalist, and advocate for Indigenous rights, has significantly contributed to sustainable development, environmental justice, and Indigenous empowerment. Her work has focused on protecting sacred lands, promoting sustainable practices, and advocating for the rights and self-determination of Indigenous communities.

LaDuke's leadership in sustainable development is rooted in her deep commitment to environmental stewardship and recognizing the interconnectedness between human well-being and the health of the natural world. She has been at the forefront of efforts to promote renewable energy, sustainable agriculture, and local self-reliance within Indigenous communities. LaDuke has advocated for the development of renewable energy sources, such as wind and solar power, as alternatives to fossil fuels, highlighting the importance of environmental sustainability and the need to address the impacts of climate change.

In her work to protect sacred lands, LaDuke has been a vocal advocate for preserving culturally significant sites and recognizing Indigenous spiritual and cultural practices. She has played a vital role in campaigns to halt destructive development projects, such as the construction of oil pipelines and mining operations, that threaten Indigenous lands and waters. LaDuke has emphasized the importance of honoring and respecting Indigenous peoples' relationship with the land, asserting that their stewardship practices can offer valuable insights for addressing global environmental challenges.

LaDuke's efforts to empower Indigenous communities economically and politically have been centered on fostering self-sufficiency, promoting sustainable economic development, and advancing Indigenous sovereignty. She has championed initiatives prioritizing local control and decision-making, encouraging sustainable business practices that preserve cultural integrity and benefit the community. LaDuke has also advocated for Indigenous rights, pushing for legal and policy reforms that protect Indigenous peoples' land, water, and treaty rights.

Through her activism and advocacy, LaDuke has been a voice for Indigenous peoples globally, highlighting the importance of Indigenous knowledge, wisdom, and perspectives in addressing the pressing issues of our time. She has worked tirelessly to raise awareness about Indigenous communities' struggles and resilience and challenge the systemic injustices they face. LaDuke's work has empowered Indigenous peoples and inspired individuals from diverse backgrounds to join the fight for social and environmental justice.

In recognition of her contributions, LaDuke has received numerous awards and honors for her activism, including the Reebok Human Rights Award and the International Slow Food Award for Biodiversity. She has also been a candidate for the Vice Presidency of the United States, representing the Green Party, further amplifying her platform and advocacy.

Buffy Sainte-Marie: Artistic Expression and Cultural Advocacy

Buffy Sainte-Marie, an Indigenous Canadian singer-songwriter, musician, and activist, has significantly contributed to the music industry, Indigenous rights advocacy, and preserving Indigenous cultures. Through her powerful music, outspoken activism, and dedication to education, she has left a lasting impact on social justice and Indigenous empowerment.

Sainte-Marie's impact on the music industry is notable for her unique blend of folk, rock, and Indigenous musical influences. Her songs tackle many themes, including love, social issues, and Indigenous rights. Known for her expressive vocals and poetic lyrics, she has captivated audiences with her talent and authenticity. In the 1960s, she emerged as a prominent voice of the era's folk music revival, garnering critical acclaim and a devoted fanbase. Her timeless songs, such as "Universal Soldier" and "Up Where We Belong," have become anthems of social consciousness.

Beyond her musical achievements, Buffy Sainte-Marie has been a fierce advocate for Indigenous rights and education. She has used her platform to shed light on the historical and ongoing injustices Indigenous communities face. Through her activism, she has raised awareness about issues such as land rights, cultural appropriation, and the need for equitable representation. Sainte-Marie has been vocal in supporting Indigenous self-determination and has called for recognizing and preserving Indigenous cultures.

One of Sainte-Marie's notable contributions to Indigenous education is the creation of the Cradleboard Teaching Project. This initiative focuses on developing culturally appropriate educational materials incorporating Indigenous perspectives and histories. The project aims to promote cultural pride and understanding among Indigenous youth while fostering cross-cultural awareness in non-Indigenous communities. Sainte-Marie's commitment to education and empowering Indigenous youth has significantly impacted bridging gaps in educational opportunities and ensuring cultural continuity.

Throughout her career, Sainte-Marie has effectively utilized her art as a platform for cultural preservation and activism. Her music often addresses Indigenous themes, highlighting Indigenous cultures' struggles, resilience, and beauty. By incorporating traditional Indigenous sounds and instrumentation into her music, she has brought attention to the richness and diversity of Indigenous musical traditions. Sainte-Marie's performances and public appearances have also provided spaces for dialogue and reflection on Indigenous issues, challenging stereotypes and promoting understanding.

Buffy Sainte-Marie's contributions to the music industry, Indigenous rights advocacy, and cultural preservation have earned her numerous accolades and honors, including the Order of Canada and multiple Juno Awards. Her impact extends beyond her artistic achievements, as she continues to be an influential figure in the fight for social justice, Indigenous rights, and the recognition of Indigenous contributions to society. Sainte-Marie's unwavering dedication to uplifting Indigenous voices and promoting cultural understanding serves as an inspiration for artists, activists, and individuals around the world.

Wilma Mankiller: Leadership and Empowerment in Cherokee Nation

Wilma Mankiller, a Cherokee activist and leader, significantly contributed to the Cherokee Nation and inspired Indigenous women in leadership roles. As the first woman elected Principal Chief of the Cherokee Nation, Mankiller dedicated her life to improving healthcare, education, and economic development within her community.

Born in Tahlequah, Oklahoma, in 1945, Wilma Mankiller grew up immersed in Cherokee culture and faced the challenges of being a Native American in a society marked by discrimination and inequality. Despite adversity, she embraced her heritage and worked tirelessly to uplift her community.

Mankiller's leadership as Principal Chief from 1985 to 1995 was transformative for the Cherokee Nation. She prioritized community development, focusing on initiatives to improve healthcare access, educational opportunities, and economic self-sufficiency. Under her leadership, the Cherokee Nation experienced significant advancements, including establishing community health clinics, expanding academic programs, and developing financial enterprises.

One of Mankiller's notable achievements was the improvement of healthcare services for the Cherokee people. She played a crucial role in establishing the Cherokee Nation Community Health Centers, which provided accessible and culturally appropriate healthcare services to the community. Mankiller recognized the importance of addressing healthcare disparities, ensuring that her people had access to quality medical care.

Another area of focus for Mankiller was education. She believed in the power of education to empower individuals and communities. During her tenure, she implemented various educational programs, including adult literacy initiatives and scholarships for Cherokee students. Mankiller understood that a solid academic foundation was vital for the future success and prosperity of the Cherokee Nation.

Mankiller's efforts also extended to economic development. She recognized the potential for economic self-sufficiency within the Cherokee community and worked to create opportunities for entrepreneurship and job creation. She spearheaded initiatives that encouraged the growth of small businesses and promoted financial stability for the Cherokee people.

Wilma Mankiller's legacy extends beyond her accomplishments as a leader and advocate. As a trailblazer for Indigenous women, she shattered glass ceilings and paved the way for future generations. Her leadership inspired Indigenous women to pursue positions of influence and authority, challenging traditional gender roles and stereotypes. Mankiller's success demonstrated that Indigenous women could be powerful agents of change and catalysts for community development.

Wilma Mankiller remained committed to preserving and promoting Cherokee culture and heritage. She emphasized the importance of maintaining strong connections to the past while embracing progress and innovation. Mankiller's leadership style was rooted in collaboration, inclusivity, and the belief that every community member had a role in its success.

Mankiller's contributions were recognized and honored by numerous awards and accolades, including the Presidential Medal of Freedom she received in 1998. However, her true impact can be seen in the lives she touched and the positive changes she brought to the Cherokee Nation. Her legacy continues to inspire Indigenous communities and women leaders worldwide, serving as a reminder of the resilience, strength, and capacity for leadership within Indigenous cultures.

Patricia Michaels: Indigenous Fashion and Cultural Revitalization

Patricia Michaels, a Native American fashion designer, has significantly contributed to revitalizing Indigenous art and culture through her innovative approach to blending traditional Indigenous aesthetics with contemporary fashion. Her work has not only redefined Native American fashion but also served as a platform for advocating for Indigenous artisans and designers.

Born and raised in Taos Pueblo, New Mexico, Patricia Michaels has deep roots in Indigenous culture and draws inspiration from her heritage. She belongs to the Taos Pueblo and Taos tribe, and her designs reflect her community's rich cultural traditions and symbolism. Michaels' fashion creations incorporate intricate beadwork, vibrant colors, and traditional motifs, infusing them with a modern and couture sensibility.

One of the key contributions of Patricia Michaels is her ability to challenge stereotypes and misconceptions about Native American fashion. Her designs have shattered the notion that Indigenous fashion is solely limited to ceremonial or historical clothing. Michaels has demonstrated that Native American fashion can be contemporary, innovative, and relevant in the modern world.

Michaels gained widespread recognition when she participated in the reality television show "Project Runway" in 2012, where she became a finalist. Her unique designs and authentic representation of her Indigenous heritage garnered attention and acclaim from the fashion industry and beyond. This platform allowed her to reach a broader audience and showcase Indigenous fashion's beauty and cultural richness.

Beyond her creative work, Patricia Michaels has strongly advocated for Indigenous artisans and designers. She has been instrumental in promoting economic opportunities and recognition for Indigenous artists in the fashion industry. Michaels has actively collaborated with Indigenous artisans to support fair trade practices and ensure their work is ethically sourced and appropriately credited.

Moreover, Michaels has used her voice and platform to raise awareness about the cultural appropriation often faced by Indigenous artists. She has been outspoken in addressing the issue and advocating for cultural respect and understanding. By educating others about the significance of Indigenous art and fashion, Michaels has helped create a greater appreciation for Indigenous communities' cultural heritage and artistic contributions.

Patricia Michaels' work has significantly impacted the fashion industry in terms of aesthetics and cultural representation. Her designs have been showcased in prestigious fashion shows and exhibitions, bringing Indigenous fashion to the forefront and challenging the prevailing Eurocentric norms. Through her creativity and innovation, Michaels has inspired other Indigenous designers and artists to explore and express their heritage through fashion.

Michaels' contributions extend beyond the fashion world, as she actively engages in community projects and cultural preservation efforts. She conducts workshops and mentoring programs to empower Indigenous youth, encouraging them to embrace their cultural identity and pursue creative endeavors.

Patricia Michaels has received numerous awards and honors for her groundbreaking work. Her contributions to the fashion industry and Indigenous art have been celebrated, and she continues to be a trailblazer and inspiration for aspiring Indigenous designers and artisans.

Part Six

Unearthing Forgotten Legacies

6.1 LOST QUEENS AND EMPRESSES

Hatshepsut: The Female Pharaoh of Ancient Egypt

Hatshepsut, one of the few female pharaohs in ancient Egypt's history, left a lasting legacy with her remarkable reign. As the fifth pharaoh of the 18th Dynasty, she defied traditional gender roles, taking on the responsibilities and authority typically reserved for male rulers. Hatshepsut's reign was marked by notable achievements, her efforts in stabilizing Egypt, and the subsequent attempts to erase her legacy after her death.

Hatshepsut ascended to the throne around 1478 BCE, following the death of her husband and stepbrother, Thutmose II. Initially serving as regent for her young stepson, Thutmose III, Hatshepsut eventually assumed the role of pharaoh herself. She adopted the full regalia of kingship, including the traditional false beard, kilt, and headdress, symbolizing her authority and legitimacy.

One of Hatshepsut's most significant achievements was her successful trade expeditions that brought wealth and valuable resources to Egypt. She organized several ambitious trading missions to lands such as Punt (modern-day Somalia), where her diplomats and traders established strong diplomatic and economic ties. These expeditions resulted in the acquisition of exotic goods, including precious woods, incense, gold, and animals, further enriching Egypt's economy and cultural heritage.

In addition to her successful trade ventures, Hatshepsut was an avid builder and undertook numerous construction projects throughout Egypt. Most notably, she commissioned the construction of her mortuary temple, the Djeser-Djeseru, which is a testament to her architectural grandeur and artistic vision. The temple, located in the complex of Deir el-Bahari in Thebes, is renowned for its stunning design and reliefs that depict Hatshepsut's divine birth and divine mandate to rule.

Hatshepsut's reign was marked by stability and prosperity, as she focused on internal reforms, promoting trade, and establishing a strong centralized government. She sought to legitimize her rule by emphasizing her divine birth and connection to the gods, presenting herself as a chosen ruler destined to bring prosperity and order to Egypt.

However, after Hatshepsut's death, her successor Thutmose III attempted to erase her from history. He ordered the defacement and destruction of her monuments and statues, possibly due to political motivations or a desire to assert his authority. Consequently, Hatshepsut's legacy remained forgotten until modern archaeological discoveries shed light on her reign.

The efforts to restore and uncover Hatshepsut's legacy have been substantial in recent decades. Archaeologists and Egyptologists have excavated and restored her monuments and have reevaluated her reign in light of newfound evidence. Today, Hatshepsut is recognized as a significant and influential pharaoh, revered for her achievements, her unique position as a female ruler, and her enduring contributions to Egyptian history.

Hatshepsut's reign serves as a testament to the power and capability of women in ancient Egypt. Despite attempts to erase her legacy, she stands as a symbol of strength, leadership, and resilience.

Wu Zetian: Empress of China's Tang Dynasty

Wu Zetian, also known as Empress Wu, holds a unique place in Chinese history as the only woman to rule China as an empress regnant. Political intrigue, ambitious reforms, and lasting impacts on Chinese culture and politics marked her life and reign.

Wu Zetian was born in 624 CE during the Tang Dynasty and entered the imperial court as a concubine of Emperor Taizong. She possessed exceptional intelligence, wit, and political acumen, which attracted the emperor's attention. After Emperor Taizong's death, Wu Zetian became a concubine of his successor, Emperor Gaozong. However, she quickly rose in influence, becoming the de facto ruler behind the scenes.

Following Emperor Gaozong's debilitating stroke, Wu Zetian seized the opportunity to consolidate her power. She assumed the title of empress dowager and, in 690 CE, proclaimed herself the sovereign ruler, establishing the Zhou Dynasty. As China's only empress regnant, Wu Zetian held supreme authority over the empire, redefining the political landscape.

Her strong governance and ambitious reforms characterized Wu Zetian's reign. She implemented policies to promote agricultural production, enhance transportation networks, and improve the welfare of the common people. She also expanded the bureaucracy, introducing merit-based civil service examinations to ensure competent officials were appointed based on their abilities rather than their social status.

Under Wu Zetian's rule, women's rights and social mobility experienced significant advancements. She appointed women to key government positions, breaking long-standing gender barriers. Wu Zetian also established educational institutions for women, allowing them to pursue knowledge and achieve social prominence.

Wu Zetian's patronage of the arts and literature left a lasting impact on Chinese culture. She supported and encouraged renowned poets and scholars, leading to a flourishing of literary and artistic endeavors during her reign. Her patronage contributed to the development of new artistic styles and the preservation of important texts.

Wu Zetian's reign was not without controversy and opposition despite her achievements. Her rise to power and how she maintained it drew criticism from Confucian scholars and traditionalists. Historical accounts often portray her as a cunning and ruthless ruler, willing to eliminate rivals and consolidate power at any cost.

After Wu Zetian died in 705 CE, the Zhou Dynasty was quickly abolished, and she was posthumously honored as Empress Wu Zetian. Subsequent Chinese dynasties sought to diminish her legacy, painting her reign as an aberration. However, modern scholars have revisited her reign and recognized her as a formidable ruler who left a lasting imprint on Chinese history.

Wu Zetian's influence on Chinese culture and politics is still evident. Her reign challenged traditional gender roles and paved the way for greater participation of women in government and society. She also introduced administrative reforms that laid the foundation for subsequent dynasties. Wu Zetian remains a controversial figure, with her reign provoking ongoing debates and discussions about her legacy.

Rani Padmini: Queen of Mewar and Symbol of Courage

Rani Padmini, also known as Padmavati, was a legendary queen of Mewar, a kingdom in medieval India. Her life and bravery have become the subject of numerous tales, poems, and folklore, symbolizing courage, sacrifice, and beauty.

Rani Padmini lived during the 13th century and is believed to have been the queen of Chittorgarh, the capital of Mewar. While historical accounts about her are limited, her bravery and sacrifice have been immortalized in various literary works, most notably in the epic poem "Padmavat" by the Sufi poet Malik Muhammad Jayasi.

One of the most famous tales associated with Rani Padmini is her role in defending her kingdom against the invasion of Alauddin Khilji, the Sultan of Delhi. According to the legends, Khilji became enamored with Padmini's beauty and sought to possess her. To protect her honor and the honor of her kingdom, Padmini, along with other Rajput women, performed the act of "jauhar" (self-immolation) to avoid falling into the hands of the invader.

The story of Rani Padmini's bravery and sacrifice has had a significant cultural impact in India. She is revered as a symbol of feminine valor, loyalty, and self-determination. Her act of jauhar, although debated by historians, has become an iconic representation of women's courage in the face of adversity.

Rani Padmini's tale has inspired numerous literature, art, and film works. Artists and poets have depicted her beauty and courage, capturing her as a timeless symbol of grace and sacrifice. Her story continues to resonate with people, particularly in the state of Rajasthan, where Chittorgarh is located, and is celebrated during festivals and cultural events.

While historical facts about Rani Padmini may be elusive, her legacy as a brave queen who stood up against invasions and defended her kingdom remains ingrained in the cultural fabric of India. Her story exemplifies the spirit of resilience, sacrifice, and unwavering commitment to honor and values. Rani Padmini's tale serves as a reminder of the enduring power of courage and the indomitable spirit of women throughout history.

Zenobia: Queen of Palmyra and Warrior Queen

Zenobia, also known as Septimia Zenobia, was a queen of Palmyra, a prominent trading city in the third century AD. Her reign marked a significant period in Palmyra's history as she expanded its territory, challenged Roman authority, and sought to establish an independent empire in the East.

Zenobia was born into a noble Palmyrene family and married Odaenathus, the ruler of Palmyra. After her husband's assassination in 267 AD, Zenobia assumed the regency for her young son, Vaballathus, and effectively became the de facto ruler of Palmyra. She swiftly embarked on a series of military campaigns to extend her influence and challenge Roman control in the region.

Under Zenobia's leadership, Palmyra expanded its territory, capturing key cities such as Egypt and parts of Asia Minor. She created a formidable army and established diplomatic alliances with neighboring powers, making Palmyra a significant regional power.

Zenobia's ultimate objective was establishing Palmyra as an independent empire free from Roman domination. She adopted the title of "Queen of the East" and sought to position Palmyra as a rival to the Roman Empire. She was known for her ambition, intelligence, and political acumen, allowing her to govern her expanding realm effectively.

However, Zenobia's aspirations brought her into direct conflict with the Roman Emperor Aurelian. In 272 AD, Aurelian launched a military campaign against Palmyra, determined to reassert Roman control. Zenobia's forces were eventually defeated despite her efforts to resist, and she was captured. Palmyra was brought back under Roman rule, marking the end of Zenobia's reign.

Although Zenobia's reign was relatively short-lived, her strong and assertive queen legacy has endured. Her military campaigns and efforts to maintain Palmyra's independence have made her a symbol of resistance against Roman hegemony. Zenobia's story has captured the imagination of historians, writers, and artists throughout the centuries, becoming the subject of numerous literary works and even inspiring the creation of statues and sculptures.

Theodora: Empress of the Byzantine Empire

Theodora, the empress of the Byzantine Empire in the sixth century, was a powerful and influential figure who left a lasting impact on politics, women's rights, and the implementation of reforms alongside her husband, Emperor Justinian I.

Theodora was born in 500 AD in Constantinople (modern-day Istanbul) from a humble background. Her father was a bear trainer in the circus, and she began her career as an actress and performer. During her time as an actress, she caught the attention of Justinian, who was then the heir to the Byzantine throne.

Theodora and Justinian married in 525 AD, and when Justinian ascended to the throne as Emperor in 527 AD, Theodora became Empress consort. Unlike many women of her time, Theodora played an active and influential role in politics, working alongside Justinian to shape the policies and reforms of the Byzantine Empire.

One of Theodora's most significant contributions was her advocacy for women's rights. She championed laws that protected women's rights, particularly those marginalized or faced societal prejudice. Theodora worked to improve the legal status of women, addressing issues such as divorce, inheritance, and property rights. She was primarily concerned with protecting women in vulnerable situations, such as those engaged in prostitution or subject to forced labor.

Theodora's commitment to women's rights went beyond legislation. She actively supported initiatives that provided women with education and employment opportunities. She established institutions that offered shelter, protection, and vocational training for women who were victims of violence or had limited means of support.

In addition to her work on women's rights, Theodora played a crucial role in implementing significant reforms. She was deeply involved in the religious and political affairs of the Byzantine Empire, influencing policies on taxation, land reform, and social welfare. Theodora's influence was particularly evident during the Nika Riots in 532 AD when she urged Justinian not to flee the city in the face of a popular uprising. Her courage and determination helped secure the survival of the Byzantine Empire.

The partnership between Theodora and Justinian was a unique and successful collaboration. Their joint efforts resulted in the codification of Roman law, known as the Corpus Juris Civilis, which served as the foundation of Byzantine legal systems and profoundly impacted European legal traditions. Theodora's perspective and input in developing the legal code helped ensure its inclusivity and fairness.

Theodora's influence extended beyond her lifetime. Her legacy as an advocate for women's rights and active political participation has made her an enduring symbol of female empowerment and leadership. Her reign challenged societal norms and demonstrated that women could play significant roles in governance and effect positive change.

Although Theodora's reign ended with her death in 548 AD, her impact on Byzantine society and the status of women persisted. Her advocacy for women's rights and her partnership with Justinian in implementing reforms left a profound mark on the history of the Byzantine Empire and serves as an inspiration for future generations.

6.2 WOMEN IN ANCIENT HISTORY: SHATTERING MYTHS

Cleopatra: Queen of Egypt and Political Strategist

Cleopatra, the last active ruler of the Ptolemaic Kingdom of Egypt, is one of history's most fascinating and influential figures. Political acumen, diplomatic endeavors, and a significant impact on the politics of the ancient Mediterranean world mark her life and reign.

Cleopatra was born in 69 BC into the Ptolemaic dynasty, a Greek ruling family that had maintained control of Egypt for centuries. As a member of the Ptolemaic dynasty, she was well-versed in the time's intricate politics and power struggles.

When Cleopatra ascended to the throne in 51 BC at 18, Egypt faced internal conflicts and external threats from the expanding Roman Empire. Cleopatra recognized the need to secure her position and maintain Egypt's independence, and she employed her intelligence and charisma to navigate the complex political landscape.

Cleopatra's most famous alliance was with Roman general and statesman Julius Caesar. In 48 BC, she traveled to Rome and established a relationship with Caesar, who provided military and political support to help her regain her throne. Their relationship went beyond political alliance, and Cleopatra became Caesar's lover, resulting in the birth of their son, Caesarion.

After Caesar's assassination in 44 BC, Cleopatra aligned herself with Mark Antony, one of Caesar's loyal generals and one of the most powerful men in Rome. Cleopatra's union with Antony solidified her influence in Roman politics and allowed her to expand her power base in the eastern Mediterranean.

Cleopatra's alliance with Antony was based on political calculations and was driven by a shared vision of creating a powerful Eastern Mediterranean empire. However, their military campaign against Octavian, Caesar's adopted heir and rival, ended in defeat at the Battle of Actium in 31 BC.

In the aftermath of the battle, Cleopatra and Antony retreated to Egypt. Recognizing the inevitability of defeat, and facing the prospect of being captured and paraded in Rome as a trophy, Cleopatra took her own life in 30 BC, purportedly by the bite of an asp.

Cleopatra's political acumen and diplomatic endeavors profoundly influenced the ancient Mediterranean world. She skillfully navigated the shifting alliances and power dynamics between Egypt, Rome, and other Eastern Mediterranean powers. Her alliances with prominent Roman figures gave her a significant role in the politics of the Roman Empire, and her presence and influence were felt far beyond the borders of Egypt.

Cleopatra's cultural impact was also noteworthy. She embraced ancient Egypt's traditions and religious practices, presenting herself as the embodiment of the divine Egyptian ruler. She actively promoted the worship of Egyptian gods and used iconography and symbolism associated with ancient Egyptian queens and goddesses to enhance her legitimacy and appeal.

Throughout history, Cleopatra has been the subject of fascination and speculation. Her reputation has been shaped by ancient accounts and later interpretations, often portraying her as a seductress and femme fatale. However, it is important to recognize her as a capable and astute ruler who navigated complex political landscapes, protecting and furthering the interests of her kingdom.

While Cleopatra's reign ultimately marked the end of the Ptolemaic Kingdom and the beginning of Roman control over Egypt, her legacy endures. Her political acumen, diplomatic endeavors, and influence on the ancient Mediterranean world have made her one of history's most captivating and significant figures.

Enheduanna: High Priestess and Earliest Known Female Author

Enheduanna, the daughter of Sargon of Akkad, was a remarkable figure in ancient Mesopotamia and is widely recognized as the earliest known female author in history. As a Sumerian high priestess, she made significant contributions to Sumerian literature, exerted religious authority, and left an enduring legacy as a literary and spiritual figure.

Enheduanna's most notable accomplishment is her literary work. She composed a collection of hymns and prayers known as the "Sumerian Temple Hymns" or "The Exaltation of Inanna." These hymns were dedicated to the goddess Inanna, the patron deity of the city of Uruk, where Enheduanna served as a high priestess. Her hymns were religious expressions and works of great artistic and poetic merit.

The writings of Enheduanna provide insights into the religious and cultural practices of ancient Sumer. Through her hymns, she celebrated the divine qualities of Inanna, exploring themes of power, love, fertility, and the cosmic order. Her literary style was characterized by vivid imagery, emotional depth, and a profound understanding of the human condition. The hymns of Enheduanna were influential in shaping the later traditions of Sumerian and Babylonian literature.

Enheduanna's position as a high priestess granted her religious authority and prominence. As the daughter of Sargon, the founder of the Akkadian Empire, she held a prestigious position allowing her to wield political and spiritual influence. As a high priestess, she played a crucial role in Uruk's religious rituals and ceremonies, ensuring the city's and its inhabitants well-being.

Her status as a female leader in a male-dominated society was significant and marked an exception to the prevailing gender norms of the time. Enheduanna's position as a high priestess demonstrated the recognition of her intellectual and spiritual capabilities, challenging the notion that women were limited to domestic or subordinate roles.

Enheduanna's legacy as a literary and spiritual figure continues to resonate today. Her hymns are considered masterpieces of ancient literature and have been studied and appreciated for their poetic beauty and theological insights. They provide a glimpse into ancient Mesopotamia's rich religious and cultural traditions.

Moreover, Enheduanna's significance as a female author and leader stands as a testament to the enduring contributions of women throughout history. Her ability to transcend the limitations imposed by societal expectations and establish herself as an influential figure in both religious and literary spheres is an inspiration.

Boudicca: Warrior Queen of the Iceni Tribe

Boudicca, also known as Boadicea, was a courageous and influential leader of the Iceni tribe, a Celtic people in ancient Britain. Her life and rebellion against Roman rule left a lasting impact and made her a symbol of resistance and national pride.

Boudicca was married to Prasutagus, the king of the Iceni, who had allied with the Romans. However, after his death, the Romans disregarded the agreement and sought to exert control over the Iceni lands. They not only confiscated the tribe's wealth but also treated Boudicca and her daughters with disrespect, subjecting them to humiliation and abuse.

Faced with the oppressive rule of the Romans, Boudicca decided to take a stand and lead her people in rebellion. She rallied the support of other tribes suffering under Roman occupation, amassing a formidable army estimated to have numbered in the tens of thousands.

Her bravery, strategic thinking, and determination characterized Boudicca's military tactics. She led her forces in a series of successful battles against the Roman legions, inflicting heavy casualties and striking fear into the hearts of the occupiers. Her forces sacked and burnt several Roman cities, including Londinium (modern-day London) and Verulamium (modern-day St. Albans).

Although Boudicca's rebellion ultimately did not drive the Romans out of Britain, her defiance and military successes sent shockwaves throughout the Roman Empire. Her revolt highlighted the discontent and resistance of the indigenous Celtic tribes against Roman domination and inspired others to resist Roman rule in various ways.

The legacy of Boudicca as a symbol of resistance and national identity has endured throughout history. Her bravery and determination in the face of oppression have made her a revered figure, representing the spirit of the Celtic people and their struggle against foreign domination. Her story has been passed down through the generations, preserving her memory as a symbol of strength and defiance.

In modern times, Boudicca continues to be celebrated as a national hero in Britain. Her statue stands proudly on the banks of the Thames River in London, a testament to her enduring legacy. She serves as a reminder of the importance of standing up against injustice and oppression.

Sappho: Poetess of Ancient Greece

Sappho, the ancient Greek poet from the island of Lesbos, is known for her lyrical expressions of love and desire, her contributions to Greek literature, and her profound influence on subsequent generations of poets.

Born around the 7th century BCE, Sappho lived during a time when the arts, especially poetry, thrived in ancient Greece. She composed her poetry in a lyrical and melodic style, often accompanied by music and dance. Although much of her work has been lost over time, fragments and references to her poems have survived, allowing us glimpses into her poetic genius.

Sappho's poetry predominantly revolved around themes of love, desire, and the complexities of human emotions. She explored the spectrum of love, from the passionate romantic to the melancholic and longing. Sappho's verses were profoundly personal and intimate, often addressing individuals by name or capturing her emotions and experiences.

One of the notable aspects of Sappho's poetry is her expression of love for both women and men, making her an iconic figure in the history of LGBTQ+ literature. Her association with the island of Lesbos has led to the term "lesbian" derived from the island's name, highlighting her significance in queer history and culture.

Vivid imagery, rich metaphors, and the use of musical devices such as rhythm and repetition characterized Sappho's poetic style. Her verses were highly emotional and evocative, capturing the essence of human experiences and the nuances of love. Her poetry often celebrated the beauty of nature, emphasized the intensity of personal connections, and explored the complexities of desire.

Although Sappho's poetry was highly regarded during her time, much of her work was lost over the centuries. Only fragments and quotations survive in the works of later authors, which attest to her lasting influence and the high regard she held. Even in fragmentary form, her poetry resonates with readers, displaying a timeless quality that transcends the boundaries of time and culture.

Sappho's influence on subsequent generations of poets and writers cannot be overstated. Her lyrical style and exploration of love and desire set a precedent for love poetry in Western literature. Her innovative language and imagery inspired countless poets from ancient Greece to today. Her impact can be seen in the works of poets such as Catullus, Ovid, and even in the modern era with poets like T.S. Eliot and Sylvia Plath, who have all drawn inspiration from her.

Beyond her poetic contributions, Sappho played a significant role in the development of Greek literature and the cultural life of ancient Greece. She established an academy for young women on Lesbos, where she taught poetry and music. This educational institution, the "Thiasos," fostered a tradition of women's literary and artistic expression.

While much of Sappho's work remains lost to history, her influence and legacy continue to resonate. She is a poetic expression pioneer, challenging societal norms and exploring the depths of human emotions. Her lyrical verses, filled with passion and sensitivity, have left an indelible mark on the world of poetry and have inspired countless generations of poets and readers to embrace the power of language and the beauty of the human experience.

Agnodice: Pioneer Female Physician in Ancient Athens

Agnodice, a remarkable figure in ancient Athens, defied societal gender norms and significantly contributed to medicine, particularly women's health. Her story sheds light on the challenges faced by women in male-dominated societies and their determination to pursue their passions and make a difference.

In ancient Athens, women had limited rights and opportunities. They were excluded from most public life and expected to focus on domestic responsibilities. However, Agnodice refused to accept these limitations and sought to pursue her passion for medicine.

According to historical accounts, Agnodice disguised herself as a man to gain access to medical education. Women were not allowed to study medicine or practice as physicians, so Agnodice took on a male identity to circumvent these restrictions. Her dedication to learning and commitment to helping others led her to become a skilled physician, specializing in women's health and obstetrics.

Agnodice's true identity was eventually discovered when her skills as a physician became widely known, and she was accused of seducing her female patients. However, instead of facing punishment or scorn, the women she treated rallied to her defense, recognizing the invaluable care she provided. They testified that Agnodice's only interest was providing medical assistance and improving women's health.

Her case became a public spectacle, drawing attention to the gender inequality in Athens and the need for female physicians. Agnodice's story challenged the notion that women were incapable of being skilled medical professionals. Her bravery and determination inspired other women to pursue medical careers and helped pave the way for future generations of female physicians.

Agnodice's impact extended beyond her practice. She advocated for women's rights to receive medical care from female practitioners, as many women felt more comfortable discussing their health concerns with someone of their gender. Her efforts challenged the patriarchal system and the entrenched gender roles that prevented women from accessing proper medical treatment.

Agnodice's story highlights the obstacles she faced in a male-dominated society. Despite her skill and dedication, she encountered resistance and prejudice due to her gender. Her experiences shed light on the struggles women in ancient Athens faced when pursuing professions outside traditional roles.

Nevertheless, Agnodice's persistence and commitment to women's health left a lasting legacy. Her bravery and determination opened doors for future generations of women to enter the medical profession. Her story continues to inspire and remind us of the importance of challenging societal norms, advocating for gender equality, and providing essential healthcare to all individuals.

Conclusion
Lessons from the Past, Inspiring the Future

Throughout this book, we have delved into the lives and stories of several remarkable women. Often overlooked or forgotten, these individuals have left an indelible mark on their respective fields, communities, and the world. Their stories have enriched our understanding of history and provided valuable lessons that can inspire and guide us as we navigate the present and shape the future.

The women we have explored demonstrate incredible strength, resilience, and determination. They defied societal norms, challenged conventions, and shattered barriers that stood in their way. From the fields of science, art, politics, sports, and beyond, these women have shown us what is possible when passion, talent, and ambition are unleashed, regardless of gender, race, or social expectations.

Their stories remind us of the power of perseverance, even in the face of adversity. We have witnessed women who persisted in the pursuit of their dreams, overcoming obstacles and making significant contributions to their fields. Their achievements serve as a testament to the human spirit and the potential for greatness within each of us.

But their impact extends beyond their accomplishments. These women have paved the way for future generations, inspiring countless others to reach for their dreams and to challenge the status quo. They have become beacons of hope, guiding us toward a more inclusive and equitable world.

Learning from the past gives us the wisdom and knowledge to shape a better future. The lessons we draw from the hidden women in history remind us of the importance of equality, diversity, and inclusivity. They inspire us to confront injustice, challenge stereotypes, and create spaces where everyone's talents and potential can flourish.

May the stories of these remarkable women serve as a catalyst for change, igniting a collective determination to break down barriers, uplift marginalized voices, and create a world where the contributions of all individuals are recognized and celebrated.

Ellie

Printed in Great Britain
by Amazon